Leigh

Leigh

My Amazing Son

He carried his disability with
grace and dignity

CHARLENE McIVER

To my husband, Phillip,
and our beautiful sons, Jason and Leigh

★ ★ ★

Published in Australia by Charlene McIver

ISBN: 978-0-6484178-0-4
ebook ISBN: 978-0-6484178-1-1

A catalogue record for this
book is available from the
National Library of Australia

NATIONAL
LIBRARY
OF AUSTRALIA

Designed by Karen Scott Book Design
Typeset by Caz Brown
Printed in Australia by IngramSpark, Melbourne

All photographs are from the author's personal collection
with the exception of:
p38 Leigh with a group from the Civil Aviation Authority's Rescue and
Fire Fighting Service, courtesy *Leader Community News*
p49 Leigh with his basketball medal, courtesy *Leader Community News*
p57 Leigh planting seedlings, courtesy Nadrasca
p111 Leigh in his electric wheelchair, courtesy Nadrasca

pp124 and 125 Revised Consensus Resuscitation Plan, reproduced with permission
pp126 and 127 Cardiopulmonary Resuscitation information Sheet, reproduced with permission

CONTENTS

PREFACE

This is an honest and personal insight into the life of a man living with a severe physical disability and his struggle for 'normality' and acceptance.

I am a mother grieving for the loss of my youngest son, Leigh, who sadly passed away suddenly in a Melbourne hospital on Friday, 14 October 2016, aged thirty-three.

His life is recounted through the pages of this book, from his birth in 1982 to his sudden passing in 2016. Writing his biography has been an extremely difficult journey for me and, through the tears, I have relived the highs and the lows of his struggle with life. Leigh's life is a reflection of how people living with a disability cope in today's society; as his mother and full-time carer, I have the honour of sharing his story and keeping his beautiful spirit alive.

I am neither an accomplished author nor a qualified medical professional. I have attempted to describe in non-professional terms the many surgical procedures and allied health services provided to Leigh over the years. Some of the photos in this book may be confronting, but this was Leigh's life and I make no apologies in showing them.

Leigh, my second son, was diagnosed with a physical disability shortly after birth. He struggled to cope every day and endured numerous medical procedures throughout his life. He was a fighter! His dream of one day living a 'normal' life, which you and I take for granted, was simple: he just wanted to go to school, get a job, drive a car and live an independent life. It wasn't much to ask for, but with his many physical limitations even everyday activities, including dressing, washing, showering, toileting, shopping and accessing transportation, were all a challenge for him.

I watched my son struggle for thirty-three years and eleven months, and was constantly in awe of his determination to succeed at everything he did. By nature, Leigh was a very gentle and quiet person. He suffered in silence and never complained, even when situations became overwhelming. Leigh just got on with his life the best, and only, way he knew how.

I hope readers will be inspired to appreciate their lives and enjoy the things most of us take for granted: good health, family, and having both the freedom and the ability to do as they wish without physical constraints.

Medical professionals may also gain insight into the arduous and endless journey experienced by a person with a disability and their carer while accessing health services.

This book is also inspired by Leigh's wish to share his story with others and, as his mother, I will continue to advocate for him to honour that wish. It is my hope that Leigh's story will have a ripple effect and bring about changes to people's perception of what being 'disabled' means.

Leigh's life was taken too soon, and I am left with anguish, heartache and emptiness. This book is Leigh's legacy.

.

CHAPTER 1

Birth and Diagnosis

Leigh Thomas McIver was born on Saturday, 20 November 1982, at 8.01 am in a small private hospital in the eastern suburbs of Melbourne, Victoria. I was twenty-nine years old and my husband, Phillip, was thirty-one. Leigh was our second child – our second son.

I had a normal, full-term pregnancy and nine hours of labour without any major complications, apart from Leigh arriving into the world face-up. He was eager to take on the world, announcing his arrival with a loud cry.

Our healthy 4.1-kilogram (9-pound 2-ounce) baby boy was here!

Phillip and I were delighted. Leigh would complete our family; here was a little brother for Jason to play and grow up with.

After the relatively short delivery, a nurse finally handed our baby boy to me. In the dimly lit delivery room, I happened to catch sight of a small patch of blood on the lower part of his back. In the excitement, I assumed this would be wiped away once he was washed and swaddled into a blanket. I'd only held him for a short moment when a nurse quickly asked me to hand him back; he was then whisked away to another room, followed by a group of concerned medical personnel.

As Phillip and I waited for them to return with our baby, we could hear muffled whispers coming from the other room. A stream of nurses came in and out of the delivery room to check on us, not saying a word or indicating anything about Leigh, except for one overzealous nurse who leaned over and hugged me, telling me that it was 'okay to cry'.

What a strange comment to make just after I had given birth. Fear and confusion started to set in; we wanted to know what was going on and why the medical staff were not communicating with us about Leigh. We just wanted answers!

Eventually we were taken to the nursery where we met our baby, who was now tightly swaddled and lying face down in a crib. He was staring out at me with his big beautiful eyes as if to say, 'Here I am, Mum. I'm scared. What's happening to me? Please hold me.' I reached in to pick him up and was abruptly told by a nurse to leave him on his tummy for now until another doctor had checked him over. Her reaction heightened my anxiety and fear – the realisation that there was something seriously wrong with our baby was beginning to dawn.

The nurses continued to fuss around Leigh, avoiding our questions. Finally one commented that a specialist doctor would speak to us shortly. What type of 'specialist' doctor were they referring to? The anguish and sickening feeling that I was somehow responsible for my son's unknown condition was overwhelming. Was this a permanent condition? Would the doctors be able to help him?

I was then taken to a private room, away from the other new mothers, and advised to rest. I spent a good deal of time hiding in the bathroom feeling nauseated, confused and exhausted, trying to prepare myself to hear what our baby's future might hold.

I emerged from the bathroom, trying to hold my composure, and discovered a group of doctors and a concerned husband all waiting for me. I could tell by their expressionless faces that the news was not good. After introductions they finally informed us that the diagnosis was spina bifida (SB).

> **Spina bifida** (Latin: 'split spine') occurs because of an abnormality of the development of the spinal cord that occurs in the first trimester of pregnancy. Within the first 4 weeks after a foetus is conceived, the backbone and membranes that cover and protect the spinal cord and spine [do] not form and close properly. This can result in an opening anywhere along the spine and may cause damage to the spinal cord and nerves. The defect may be associated with a protrusion of the membrane covering the spinal cord (meninges) alone, called meningocele, or some neural elements, called a meningomyelocele. Or the defect may not be noticed until later in life.
>
> Spina bifida can cause physical and mental disabilities ranging from mild to severe, depending on the size and location of the opening in the spine, and whether the spinal cord and nerves are affected.[1]

The medical team continued to talk about Leigh's diagnosis and discuss his long-term prognosis. He would have difficulty walking and may later need to use callipers or a wheelchair. He would have bladder and bowel incontinence and may have some learning

---

1   'Spina Bifida: Condition Information', US Department of Health and Human Services, <https://www.nichd.nih.gov/health/topics/spinabifida/conditioninfo/default>.

difficulties. I don't think we ever asked or were told about his life expectancy or what 'type' of SB Leigh had; in hindsight, we were just trying to absorb what was happening with our baby and get our heads around this condition.

My head was spinning; I found it very difficult to accept and understand what the doctors were saying. It felt as though I were under water, watching someone else's life playing out in front of me. I was a spectator observing from afar.

Spina bifida: what did this mean for Leigh and our family? How could this happen? I vaguely remembered reading something about it during my first pregnancy, but never closely looked into the condition or its effects. I was completely in the dark and unprepared for this diagnosis. Self-blame, pity and guilt consumed me. I kept thinking back over my pregnancy for any illnesses I'd had or medications I might have taken that could have been a contributing factor. Phillip and I then focused on genetic predispositions that we were aware of, but nothing came to mind. Neither of our families had ever mentioned any birth disorders – although, growing up in the '60s, these issues were rarely discussed and we therefore had no real way of knowing.

Thirty-three years ago, prenatal testing was not as advanced as it is today. I had had the usual ultrasound scans along with urine and blood tests, and everything was normal. I was young and healthy and, because this was my second pregnancy, my doctor (a GP) did not recommend any additional tests – amniocentesis testing was uncommon then.

My understanding of amniocentesis testing is that a sample of amniotic fluid surrounding the foetus is extracted using a needle inserted into the uterus. Levels of alphafetoprotein (AFP) are checked for neural tube defects and other chromosomal problems. Through my own research I discovered that it is normal to have a small amount of AFP in the amniotic fluid, but levels are elevated if there is an open neural tube defect, which lets AFP leak into the amniotic sac. This means the skin that would normally cover the baby's spine is not present.

Leigh's doctors later advised us that even if an amniocentesis test had been performed the results may have been inconclusive. There was a fine membrane covering the damaged area of Leigh's spinal cord that may have prevented an accurate reading of AFP levels.

In those days, we were also unaware that a deficiency in folate or folic acid (vitamin B9) could increase the risk of babies being born with a neural tube defect, such as SB.

> **Folic acid**, taken in supplement form starting at least one month before conception and continuing through the first trimester of pregnancy, greatly reduces the risk of spina bifida and other neural tube defects.[2]

More recent reports indicate that women with a deficiency in vitamin B12 (cobalamin) may have a higher chance of delivering a baby with brain or spinal cord defects.

> **Vitamin B12** is an important vitamin for maintaining healthy nerve cells and it helps in the production of DNA and RNA, the body's genetic material. Vitamin B12 works closely with

---

2   'Spina Bifida' 2018, Mayo Foundation for Medical Education and Research, <https://www.mayoclinic.org/diseases-conditions/spina-bifida/symptoms-causes/syc-20377860>.

vitamin B9 (more commonly known as folate or folic acid),
to help make red blood cells and to help iron work better in
the body.[3]

The day after the birth, one of the specialists advised us that
Leigh would require immediate surgery to close the opening on
his back. I was horrified. What type of surgery? What opening on
his back? How much damage is there to the area and what does it
look like? I hadn't had a chance to look closely at his back before
he was taken away, so I had no idea what they were referring to.
Questions flooded my mind and, instinctively, all I wanted to do
was hold and nurse him.

Phillip started to cry, which I'd never seen him do before. I was
still in a state of shock and denial, and became very frustrated
and angry with his reaction. In my mind, Leigh would get better,
come home with us, and convince these doctors their diagnosis was
incorrect.

As the days passed, Leigh's diagnosis started to sink in; my
mind raced with feelings of guilt, anger and fear. I remember telling Phillip that if he wanted to walk away from our marriage,
I would completely understand. I began to realise that our lives
would never be the same and it was going to take a huge amount
of work, love and commitment to help our baby live a normal life.
Phillip turned to me with a perplexed expression and told me that
he loved me and our sons, and that no one was to blame – we would
get through this together as a family. We never spoke about who

---

3   'Spina Bifida' 2018, Mayo Foundation for Medical Education and Research,
    <https://www.mayoclinic.org/diseases-conditions/spina-bifida/symptoms-causes/
    syc-20377860>.

was 'to blame' again, but I continued to carry feelings of overwhelming guilt for many years.

Those mixed feelings were later transformed into a drive and determination to ensure Leigh received the best medical care available, and that I would be there with him to make it happen.

As Leigh grew older we would often talk about his birth and his disability. He would say to me, 'I don't blame you for my disability, Mum, and I know you love me!' It would break my heart to hear him say these words and to forgive me, his mother.

His beautiful, unselfish nature inspired me and made me even more determined to fight for him throughout his life. I would be his voice; and my love for him would be the driving force that would ensure he received everything he deserved to make his life a little easier.

However, nothing could have prepared us for the difficult and relentless journey that lay ahead for Leigh.

CHAPTER 2

First Surgery and Coming to Terms

The following day Leigh was transferred by ambulance from the small private hospital in the eastern suburbs to a large public hospital in the city centre of Melbourne, where he was to have the back closure surgery. It would be the first of many surgeries to come. I followed later that day.

He was admitted into ICU and I was sent to a private room on another floor of this huge hospital. I was feeling extremely anxious and even became slightly delusional. I believed the medical team looking after Leigh intentionally wanted to keep us apart because they knew his condition was grim and that his back surgery would not go well. I was convinced they had separated us to prevent me from forming a maternal bond with my baby!

At this stage, Phillip was at home looking after Jason, our two-year-old son. I was on my own; feeling very isolated in an unfamiliar environment and fearful about Leigh's pending surgery.

The night before his surgery, a nurse offered me some pain relief to help me sleep; she could see I was very anxious and having trouble settling. I took the medication and just as I was drifting off to sleep, I felt the bed suddenly shake violently! I thought to myself, 'What sort of medication did she give me?' I discovered that Melbourne had experienced an earthquake of 5.4 magnitude during the night, which came from Wonnangatta Valley, 200 kilometres north-east of Melbourne. Was this a sign? I am not a superstitious person, but it certainly gave me a scare and heightened my already nervous state of mind.

My parents came into the hospital later that day to visit us. My father, a strong-willed man, burst into tears while hugging me. He told me that they were there to support us and if we ever needed any help, we only had to ask. My mother then spoke over my father in an attempt to interrupt his emotional outburst by shifting the conversation towards some trivial matter. This was her way of coping with stress.

My parents were good, honest, hard-working people who grew up during the Great Depression. They were taught to be prudent with money and reserved with their feelings; this was the Victorian way. My two sisters and I were raised in a happy and safe environment; we learned to respect and appreciate the things we had, and to never take anything for granted. We were taught to work hard and always save for that 'rainy day', to be prepared for whatever life might throw at us. These were wise lessons for which I am truly grateful. Sadly, I lost my father in 1991 and my mother passed away a year later; both were in their mid-eighties. I still miss them dearly.

My family had never been closely involved with anyone with a disability, so it was difficult for them to understand what was happening to their daughter and grandson. Leigh's diagnosis was rarely discussed in any detail within the family, but I came to accept this as their way of protecting us from further stress and anxiety.

Unfortunately, I found their well-meaning approach disheartening and frustrating, and it did little to help alleviate the sense of remorse and fear I was feeling at the time.

Before Leigh was due to have his back closure surgery, we were asked by his neurosurgeon if we wanted to proceed with the closure and told that we had a choice! I cannot remember anyone mentioning a 'choice' to us previously, or explaining what would happen if he didn't have the surgery. We were advised that if we chose not to proceed, Leigh would be made comfortable, fed and monitored. The surgeon also added, in not so many words, that his life expectancy would be considerably shortened without the procedure.

Phillip and I were both a little surprised at the surgeon's question and statement. Perhaps the doctors had mentioned this when they explained Leigh's diagnosis to us, I just could not recall. We were both determined to give our baby every chance of survival and we quickly answered, 'Yes, please go ahead with the surgery and do everything you possibly can!'

Some hours later, we were told his surgery had gone as well as could be expected. I sat next to Leigh in the neonatal intensive care unit, watching and listening to him breathe, thinking about the ordeal he'd just been through so soon after his birth. Would he pull through and live a healthy life? What would his life be like? How would he cope? And how would our family cope? My precious boy was laying there on his tummy in a deep sleep, oblivious to the turmoil that lay ahead of him.

I left hospital later that day, still in shock, feeling exhausted and empty. Returning home without your newborn baby is every new mother's fear. But I had Jason at home, waiting for his mother, and I gathered some strength through his love, hugs and kisses. We visited Leigh every day that he was in hospital. I can still remember anxiously pushing through the heavy plastic doors leading into the neonatal unit, smelling the disinfectant and hearing the sounds of newborn babies crying out for their mothers. It broke my heart every time. The loudest cry I came to recognise was my *own* baby's. The nurses would try to alleviate our stress by joking about his strong pair of lungs and how beautiful he was. Looking back on those light-hearted comments now, I think how ironic it is that those strong lungs would eventually fail him later in life.

We lived an hour away from the hospital; it was difficult travelling each day and leaving Jason with relatives. I'm sure it was difficult for him to understand what was going on, and why his mother was always in tears and disappearing on him. We've talked about those years and he has some recollections of that time, but to him nothing appeared out of the ordinary. That was good to hear because I had feared that he would be resentful of his little brother because of my reactions or any comments he overheard. I wanted Jason to have a happy childhood and not form negative memories of his little brother even before he had come home.

We took pictures of Leigh after the surgery and tried to behave like 'normal' parents celebrating the birth of their baby. But everything wasn't fine. I fought back tears every day and avoided other people so that I didn't have to answer difficult questions.

I remember a doctor commenting to me that I was 'grieving for the baby I thought I was having and learning to accept the baby I now had'. I thought about this for a moment – it sounded like a phrase straight out of a psychology textbook – and found it difficult to compare my feelings with this interpretation. I was not grieving

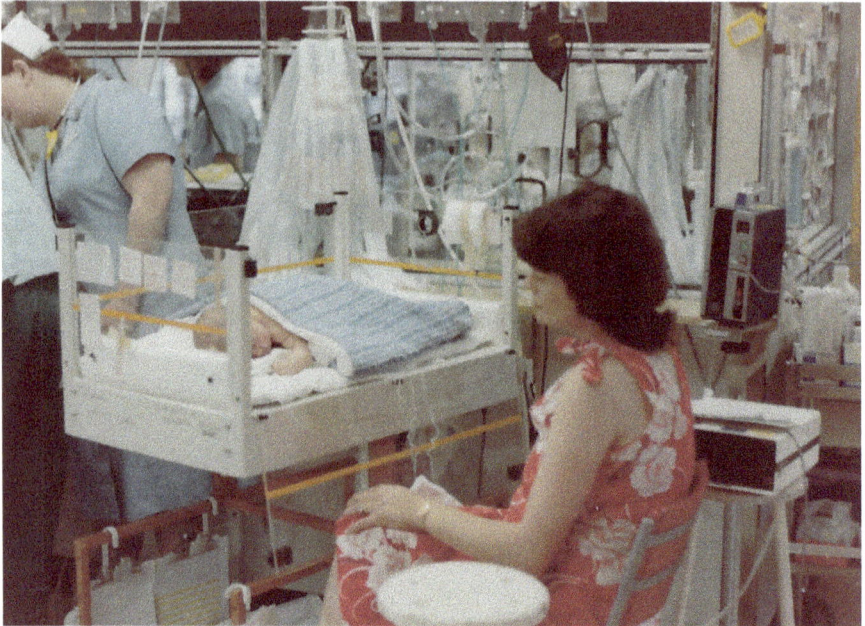

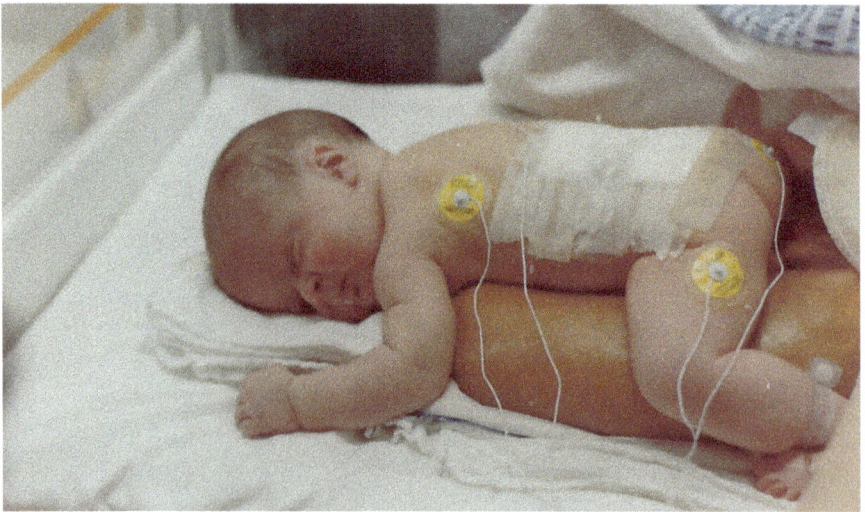

Leigh and I in ICU, just after his back closure surgery in November 1982.

for the baby I thought I was going to have and lost; I was grieving over the *condition* Leigh was born with and the difficulties that lay ahead for him. Leigh was not the disability!

Phillip and I shared our innermost fears and thoughts with each other about every aspect of Leigh's life. We both wanted him to have the best possible chance of survival and live a good life. Phillip was my rock, always there to support and comfort me, and acknowledge my anger and frustrations.

CHAPTER 3

More Surgery and Difficult Times Ahead

A few days after Leigh's back closure surgery, and while he was still recovering in ICU, his head slowly began to swell. We were told he now had hydrocephalus (increased pressure inside the skull from accumulated cerebrospinal fluid) and was being monitored closely. We were referred to a doctor who specialised in treating children and babies with SB; he would explain what was happening to Leigh and prepare us for future treatments.

Leigh's condition was considered severe (the medical terminology is myelomeningocele), although I do not remember hearing this word mentioned when he was born. I do remember doctors classifying the lesion on his spine as L5 (lower lumbar).

The specialist calmly explained that Leigh needed a ventriculoperitoneal shunt (VP shunt) to regulate and drain the excess cerebrospinal fluid from the ventricle in his brain into his abdomen (peritoneal cavity), where it would be absorbed.

He went into detail about what the device looked like and what it was made of; he drew a picture to show how it would work. He explained where the shunt would be placed on Leigh's head under the skin, and how a tube would run from the shunt into his abdomen to drain. It felt as if he were talking about someone else's baby. I kept telling myself that Leigh didn't need the shunt and that he would get better and come home with us. However, as Leigh's head continued to swell the VP shunt surgery became a necessity.

He was scheduled for his second surgery less than a week after the back closure and, thankfully, everything went well again. He healed amazingly quickly – my brave, beautiful boy – and after more time recovering in ICU, our precious baby finally came home.

Leigh now had half of his hair shaved off and a large scar on the back of his head towards one side, as well as the original scar on his back, and a scar just below his rib cage where the shunt drainage tube had been inserted.

I was both excited and apprehensive about bringing him home. I had no medical training and was concerned as to how I would cope with all his needs after the professional care he had received since birth. We were told by a nurse to just treat him like a 'normal' baby and everything would be fine. That would be easy, I thought. I had already raised my first baby, how hard would this be? How unprepared I was for what lay ahead!

I was unable to breastfeed Leigh following his birth due to stress and the distance we had to travel each day, which was very disappointing for me. It robbed me of our bonding time together, which I had enjoyed with Jason. Leigh was our little 'stranger' coming home with us. Phillip and I were looking forward to settling back into 'normal' family life and getting acquainted with our second son, and for Jason to finally meet his little brother face-to-face.

* * *

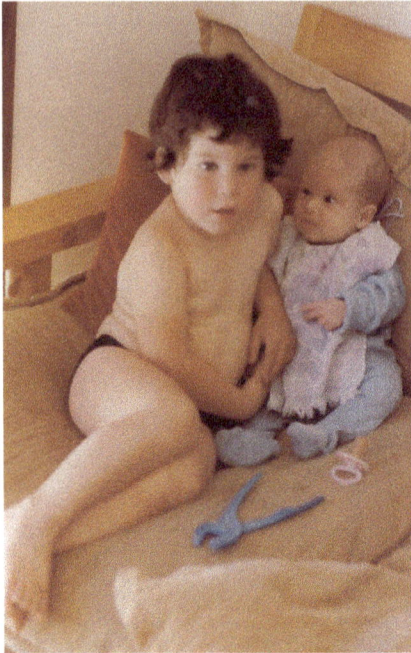

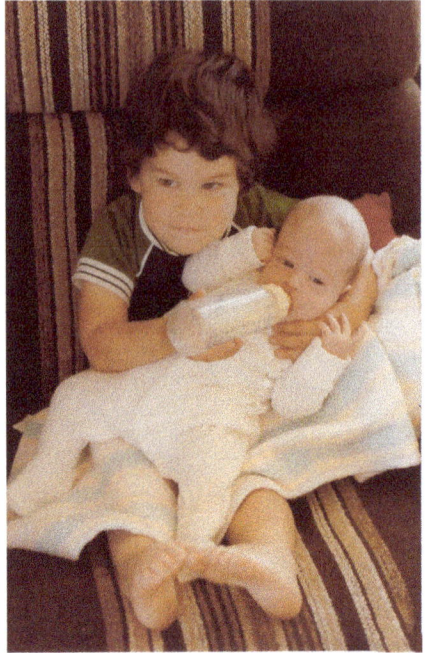

Jason and Leigh getting acquainted, early 1983. RIGHT: Big brother helping with bottle feeding.

Family support was not always possible. My parents were elderly (both were in their seventies) and did not live nearby. My older sister Denise, who had her own young family to raise, would help out whenever possible, and my oldest sister Sylvia, who was some years senior to me, also lived far from us. Phillip's parents had both passed away before our children were born, but he had aunts, uncles and cousins who we would see from time to time – they were a great source of support.

Leigh accepted bottle feeding and formula and was an excellent sleeper, however, bath time was often a challenge. Because he did not have any bowel or bladder control, it was sometimes a struggle to keep him in clean water, both as an infant and as a child.

I tried not to compare Leigh's care with Jason's and eventually realised that Leigh's needs were going to require a unique approach. Small issues around his general care and wellbeing were never touched on during any of our hospital visits, and I often felt overwhelmed and ill-equipped to cope with all his needs. It took many years for me to stop being so hard on myself and to accept that things were different this time and just enjoy time with Leigh.

We had been told by the specialists that Leigh would likely have limited use of his legs. During those early days it was difficult to determine how much sensation he had below the waist. Paraplegia was never mentioned. We would tentatively watch his legs and feet for any sign of voluntary movement. Occasionally they would jump when being tickled, but we eventually came to acknowledge that this was an involuntary reflex and our hopes sank.

Gradually we came to accept Leigh's limitations and learned to be watchful over his legs, feet and toes, protecting them from getting stuck, grazed or sunburnt, as well as alerting others who were with him to also be mindful.

His care and wellbeing was an ongoing learning experience and I just did the best I could with the resources I had: willpower and determination. I was going to raise a healthy baby and not focus on the disability!

★   ★   ★

It wasn't long before Leigh became unwell. The site of his VP shunt swelled to the size of a golf ball and he started to vomit. We rushed him into the hospital Emergency Department, where they advised us that the shunt was blocked and needed to be surgically replaced.

Aged around nine months of age supported in a special canvas seat and table for playtime in hospital.

After the revision surgery things settled down at home again. As Leigh grew up and started to eat solid foods, it was usual for him to suddenly choke, which in turn made him gag and often vomit. He would sit at the dinner table continually chewing food that he found tough – especially meat – until it became a hard ball that he could not swallow. It was almost a dinner-time ritual for him and it caused a great deal of stress for everyone at the table. I would see the frustration on his face from not being able to swallow the food. He was also eager to please me and it would all become too much for him, ending in tears. Of course, I would give in and tell him to take the meat out of his mouth and eat the rest of his dinner!

So mealtimes were sometimes unsettling for everyone. Looking back on those episodes now, I can only relate this to his little body reacting or adjusting to the shunt. I can still remember Jason at about the age of three running into the laundry to fetch a bucket every time Leigh coughed at the table. When the boys were older we would joke about Jason springing into action with 'bucket duty'. Although it was not funny or pleasant for anyone at the time, later they could see the humorous side of those days. We were all learning to overcome the difficulties and move forward.

As he grew older, Leigh's favourite food was pasta, especially spaghetti Bolognese and lasagne. I would make these from scratch, even mincing up lean steak, to reduce the amount of fat and salt in his diet. It was good to see him enjoy his food without all the tears. It was also a way of getting some iron into his diet without causing any more stress at mealtimes. He eventually outgrew his 'food phobia' and was able to eat meat and other tough foods without any problems.

Over the following months, there were numerous shunt revisions, hospital stays and constant travelling. Doctors were at a loss as to why the shunts kept failing. Leigh was eventually diagnosed as having an allergic reaction to either the silicone or the latex used during the manufacture of the device. An alternative material was trialled on a subsequent shunt revision, which finally proved successful.

I have since learned that sensitivity to latex can be a common problem for people with SB because they are exposed to it so frequently: latex gloves worn by medical personnel; anaesthetic equipment; latex tubing; catheters, and much more. These products come in direct contact with the skin or mucous membranes, such as the mouth, eyes, genitals, bladder or rectum. Serious reactions can also occur if latex enters the bloodstream. In addition, powder (for example, on latex gloves or balloons) that has absorbed latex particles can become airborne and be inhaled.

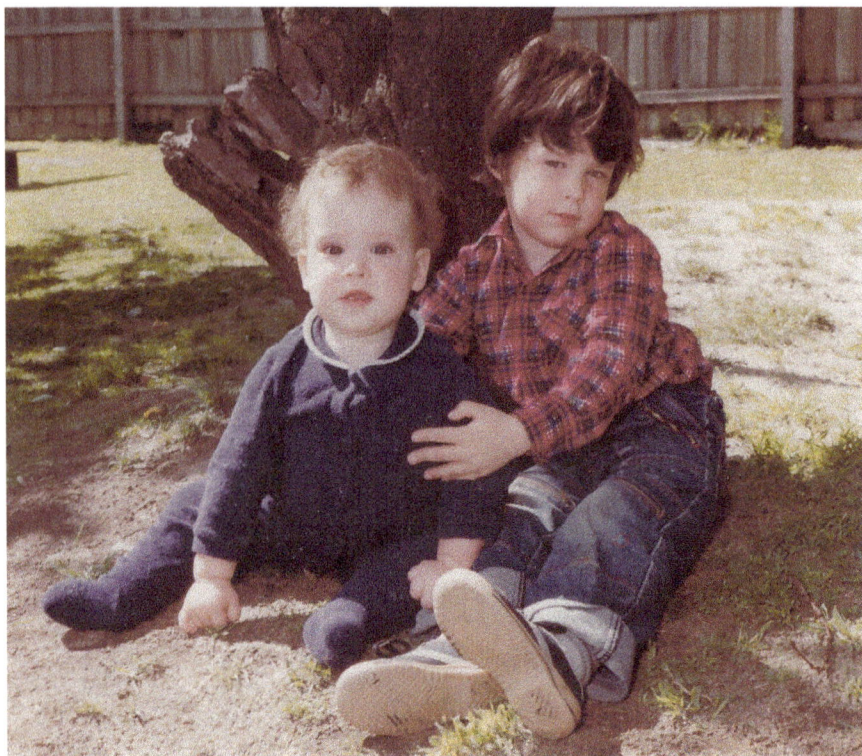

Our boys in 1984, with Jason, aged three, supporting his brother Leigh, aged sixteen months.

Leigh would come home from birthday parties with swollen eyes and mouth. Initially, I thought this was caused by a food allergy, but eventually I realised it was an allergic reaction to the powder on the balloons. Fortuntely, he outgrew this allergy.

Finally, things settled down again. We were getting to know our second son, and his personality began to shine through. He was a very easygoing and amazingly happy baby, considering what he'd been through, and he had a lot of love to share with his parents and brother. He was interested in everything around him and quickly caught up with home life, toys, pets and just having fun.

Leigh was unable to sit without support; he would lean to one side and rest on his arm or hold on to an object to steady himself. He would sometimes try to sit unaided and often fall over on to his back, ending up with his feet in the air. We would all hold our breath and wait for a cry, but he would pull himself back up with a big smile on his face, which would make us all laugh!

*   *   *

It was some months later, during a school run to collect Jason, that Leigh became unwell again. He vomited, started to shake and became unresponsive. I panicked and drove like a mad woman to the local doctor's surgery, where he was diagnosed as having had a grand mal (severe) epileptic seizure. He was later transferred by ambulance and admitted to hospital for observation.

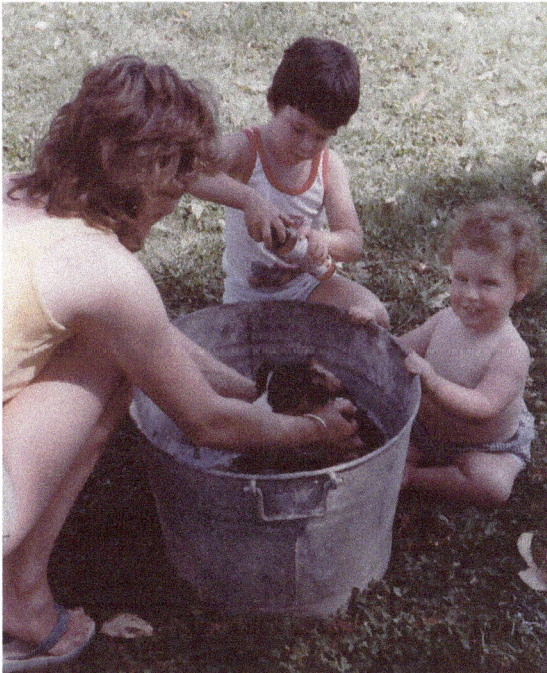

Our boys helping to bathe Charlie, our cavalier King Charles spaniel. Leigh, with his cheeky smile, is about eighteen months old and Jason, in charge of the shampoo, is about three-and-a-half years old.

Leigh's epilepsy would be managed through medication for the rest of his life. It took trial and error with different medications to find the one with least side effects. The one we finally settled on still made him appear a little sedated and gave him a slight tremor in his hands, but he tolerated it well. As he grew older the dosage was increased from one 250-milligram tablet per day to one 500-milligram tablet three times per day. We made sure he took his medication religiously. If doses were missed or not properly ingested because of illness, he could have an occasional seizure.

At such a young age, he was not able to indicate to me the onset of a seizure, so we were sometimes taken by surprise. I quickly learned to read the signs and prepare us both for the onset.

Some absence episode seizures (petit mal) were brief, lasting only seconds, with symptoms that were difficult to read such as 'blanking out' or staring into space. The more severe seizures (grand mal) would contort his body with uncontrollable muscle spasms. He would drool or froth at the mouth, lose consciousness and sometimes vomit afterwards. These would last only two or three minutes, but it seemed like an eternity! Once the convulsions stopped, he would be confused and completely exhausted, and would then sleep for some hours. When he was older, Leigh was able to recognise the warning signs of either flashing lights in his eyes or blurred vision and tell me that a seizure was about to happen.

This was an extremely stressful time for both of us and for anyone who witnessed the seizures. I was always mindful of how long one could last before I needed to seek medical assistance, but fortunately I never had to.

After investigation, the neurosurgeon decided that the single VP shunt was insufficient, so a second shunt was surgically implanted

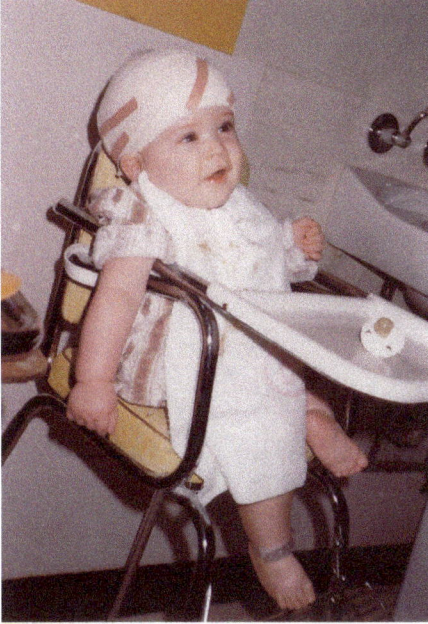

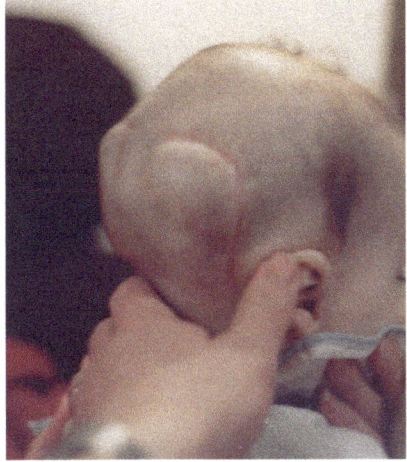

LEFT: Leigh sitting in a hospital highchair after a shunt revision, still managing a smile. ABOVE: Hair shaved from prior surgeries, showing both shunts swollen again.

on the other side of Leigh's head. Despite this, Leigh continued to have similar blockages; sometimes both devices would become blocked simultaneously. His neurosurgeon, Miss Elizabeth Lewis, later commented that Leigh was one of her most difficult cases.

Leigh spent more time in hospital and then came back home again to get on with family life.

Due to the numerous shunt revisions, his scalp was crisscrossed with thick scars, which his hair would never grow over or cover. Sometimes when we were out people would stare at Leigh, but it never seemed to worry him.

★   ★   ★

I was raising an energetic two-year-old and a young baby with special needs; a few years later I re-entered the workforce on a part-time basis to help pay our mortgage. I was determined to do it all

Pictured in 1990, Jason aged ten and Leigh aged eight.

on my own. Looking back now, I'm not sure how I coped! We had no friends or family to offer assistance on a daily basis, although from all outside appearances it probably seemed as though we were coping. In reality it was an enormous strain on all of us.

It was very important to me that my boys would be able to play together and bond. Jason was very active and loved to ride his bike, climb and play sports; Leigh was happy to sit back, play with toys and watch his brother. In their younger days I would try to spread my attention between them and their different interests in an effort to ensure neither one felt neglected or overlooked.

Over time, however, I came to realise that my sons had completely different personalities and that I didn't have to try so hard to bring them together. As they grew older, they found common interests on their own through their love of computers, electronic games and much more.

CHAPTER 4

Clinics, New Equipment and Orthopaedic Surgery

It was back in 1983 when we started to take Leigh to a monthly Spina Bifida clinic at a large hospital in the city centre of Melbourne. The clinic was held on a Saturday morning, which made it convenient for working parents, but traveling into the city with two small children was difficult. The SB clinic later relocated in 1987 to a new hospital in the south-eastern suburbs. This move made it much easier for us with the shorter traveling distance.

At this clinic Leigh was seen by a team of specialists: orthopaedist, urologist, neurosurgeon, physiotherapist, paediatrician and others. They were long and exhausting sessions and it was sometimes stressful listening to the specialists and therapists talk about Leigh's long-term prognosis and the various treatments he may or may not require. We were also able to speak with other parents about their experiences; and to watch the children use their wheelchairs or callipers, and to see how they interacted with each other.

It became obvious to us then that Leigh's condition was far more pronounced than most; I think Leigh also started to notice this as he got older. He would sometimes prefer to sit with us at the clinics rather than interact and play with the other children.

The SB clinic appointments could be daunting. Leigh was getting all the attention and making sure Jason did not feel neglected or overlooked was also difficult. So after the clinic we would treat the children to a takeaway lunch of their choice and try to put all the medical issues and stress aside – for a short time, anyway.

Leigh also had strabismus (wandering or crossed eyes) where one of his eyes (or sometimes both) would drift to one side, making him appear cross-eyed. This was more obvious when he was tired, about to have a seizure or just unwell. After numerous visits to the hospital outpatients ophthalmology clinic – and wearing an eye patch on either eye for weeks at a time – it was decided that the only way to resolve this was with corrective surgery on both eyes.

We later discovered his strabismus was most likely associated with the hydrocephalus; at the SB clinic we noticed this was a common condition in the children who had shunts.

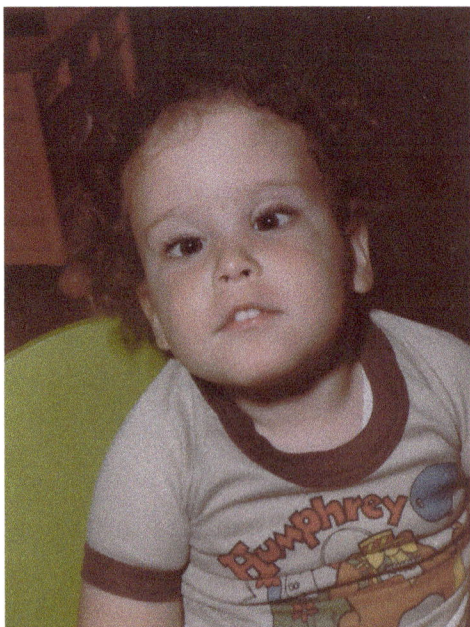

Leigh, about two years old, before the corrective eye surgery, showing the strabismus condition.

Although the condition was surgically corrected when Leigh was about two years old, his eyes would still occasionally wander when he was unwell or overtired. He learned to correct this himself by focusing on an object in order to align his eyes.

I was conscious that Leigh was not always reaching his childhood development markers. He had poor eye–hand coordination and sometimes had problems remembering and processing information in the short term. He also loved listening to music. I hoped that combining these two areas might improve these cognitive skills so when he was about three years old I enrolled him for Suzuki piano lessons, which involves repeatedly listening to a piece of music and then recalling it. Leigh enjoyed the lessons and became very accomplished, but unfortunately they were postponed indefinitely due to frequent hospital appointments and surgeries.

★　★　★

Leigh was about two or three years old when we were shown by a nurse how to catheterise him to help keep him relatively dry (for up to three or four hours at a time) in preparation for when he started kindergarten. He took over the intermittent self-catheterisation when he was in primary school, initially with the assistance of a visiting district nurse until he was proficient at managing it on his own.

> A **catheter** is a thin, clean hollow tube which is usually made of soft plastic or rubber. Urinary catheterisation means to introduce a catheter into the bladder to inject or remove fluid. A urinary catheter can give a person control over their bladder and keeps them dry.[4]

4　'Urinary Catheterisation' 2015, BetterHealth, Victoria State Government, <https://www.betterhealth.vic.gov.au/health/conditionsandtreatments/urinary-catheterisation>.

Teaching Leigh about personal hygiene as a child was an ongoing exercise in order to prevent urinary tract infections (UTIs). He frequently had UTIs that sometimes made him quite sick, with high temperatures and vomiting. Later, as an adult, he had to take a continual course of antibiotics as a preventative measure.

Almost all people born with SB have bowel problems because of damaged nerves at the base of the spinal cord. The nerve damage affects three areas of the bowel: the external anal sphincter; the sensory mechanism that tells the brain when the rectum is full; and the muscles that move the faeces along the colon and out of the body.

As Leigh grew older, his bowel care regime involved a 'bowel wash' or 'irrigation' procedure, which consisted of a plastic drainage bag and a rectal catheter to introduce warm water into the bowel.

These bowel washes proved to be extremely messy and stressful for Leigh, as well as time consuming. He'd usually end up in tears or vomiting from straining too hard to dislodge the impacted stools. The procedure was carried out over the toilet with the bag of warm water raised above the toilet and a soft catheter inserted a few centimetres into the rectum to flush out the stools. This procedure sounds good in theory, but it was difficult for Leigh to balance and feel safe on the toilet, and then to push. I resorted to laying him down in an empty bathtub so he would feel more at ease, but this was a messy procedure and usually unsuccessful.

He eventually ended up with a hernia in his groin from the straining, which ultimately required corrective surgery. It was a constant learning exercise for me to regulate his bowel movements, keep him calm during the process and, more importantly, keep him clean between toilet sessions. It was also extremely important to him as he grew older that he not be embarrassed by having 'little accidents', especially at school.

My solution was a 'manual' bowel evacuation, which was much easier, less stressful and quicker for both of us. This involved the removal of faecal matter with my gloved hand while he was sitting over the toilet. We did this on a daily basis until I felt he could go for longer periods of time without having an accident. It was less invasive and solved many problems. At this stage we also had a support frame around the toilet, which helped Leigh feel more at ease.

I also regulated Leigh's diet to help keep him relatively clean between toilet sessions. I reduced the quantity of high-fibre foods while still ensuring that he had a wide variety of fruit and vegetables. This diet is not one I would recommend for everyone, but it suited Leigh. He remained regular, clean, healthy and, above all, happy!

★   ★   ★

Leigh's first mode of transport, from when he was about ten months old, was a little green chariot on loan through a hospital. It was a high-backed wooden trolley that sat low to the ground. The large wheels at the back and smaller castors at the front made it look like an oversized skateboard. He would propel himself around the house, often bumping into furniture and thoroughly enjoying this new sense of independence. He graduated into his first wheelchair when he was about four years old.

When he was about two, Leigh started to wear small, custom-made callipers, which fitted into wool-lined, leather boots. The callipers provided support for his joints, which enabled him to

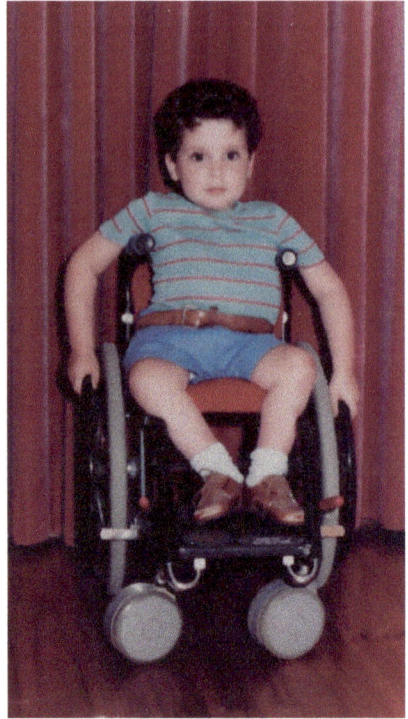

LEFT: Leigh, about two years old, trying out his new callipers with Jason, Charlie (our puppy) and me. RIGHT: Sitting in his first wheelchair in 1986, aged four. He loved the independence and freedom it gave him.

stand for the first time. He was delighted, but also very nervous! Although Leigh did not have the upper body strength or ability to swing his legs through in order to move forward, the callipers did help prevent contracture (shortening and hardening of muscles, tendons and other tissues) and to straighten his legs.

Leigh only had control over the upper half of his body, so he needed a great deal of help and encouragement to learn to balance in a standing position. He would only stand for short periods of time, aided by a frame or when holding onto something, and his fear of falling would sometimes be so overwhelming that he would end up in tears.

As Leigh grew older, the technicians at the major hospital in Melbourne developed a 'swivel walker' in an effort to keep him standing and mobile. This custom built orthotic equipment helped to support him upright; it provided rigid support across his knees and chest in order to compensate for lack of muscle control. Shifting his weight from side to side by moving his shoulders was enough to move the walker forward. However, Leigh didn't have confidence using the walker and was afraid of falling so he would also hold on to either walking sticks, a frame or his wheelchair.

Raising Leigh into a standing position was extremely beneficial, not only to support his weak joints, but also to improve the function of his pulmonary and digestive systems, and to provide weight-bearing activity that, in turn, would increase his bone mineral density. Most importantly for Leigh, he could now engage with his peers at eye level.

However, despite all our encouragement to continue standing and using the swivel walker, he still could not overcome the constant fear of falling and would sometimes be inconsolable. Therefore, we did not persevere and he eventually outgrew the walker, which was then returned to the hospital with our appreciation.

★ ★ ★

Leigh's scoliosis started to develop at a young age (at around four or five years). To help control this, he had to wear a small plastic moulded vest (or brace) lined with firm felt. Leigh's form of scoliosis was later identified as kyphoscoliosis, which is a combination of outward curvature (kyphosis) and lateral curvature (scoliosis), of the spine. The vest was shaped like a small, sleeveless jacket that came around his rib cage and was fastened with velcro straps at

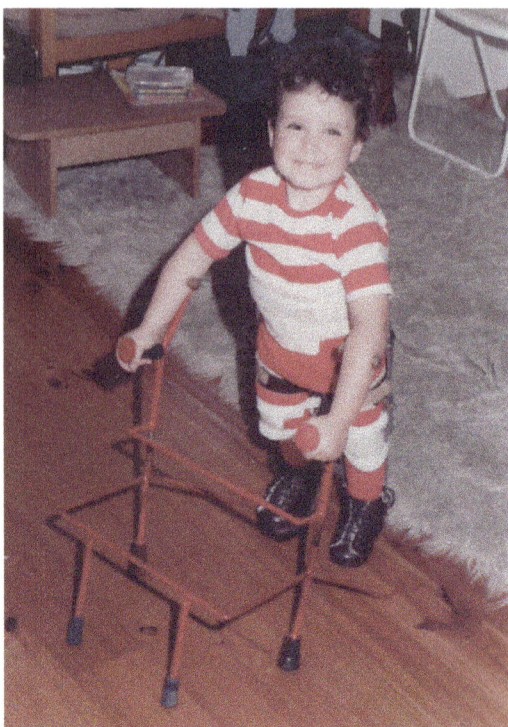

LEFT: Putting on a brave face wearing his callipers. Aged around three years.

RIGHT: Nervously trying out his swivel walker at primary school. Next to the wall is the special table he would stand at to free his hands when doing schoolwork.

the front. It gave him some degree of support while sitting, but unfortunately the plastic made Leigh sweat and he developed a pressure ulcer on his back. Despite this, he wore the vest every day for many months without complaint.

Leigh would frequently develop pressure wounds or ulcers from ill-fitting orthotic equipment or seating systems that he had outgrown. Sadly, recurring skin ulcers would be a problem throughout his life.

★   ★   ★

Leigh had to have many corrective orthopaedic surgeries during his childhood – on his knees, legs, hips and spine – in order to maintain a good sitting position.

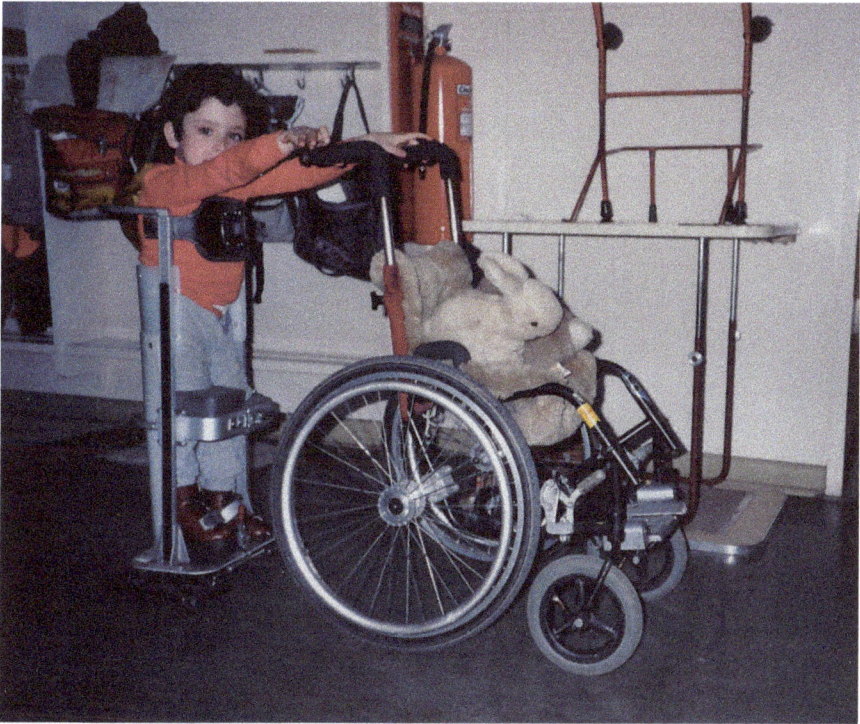

In September 1991, Leigh (aged nine) underwent orthopaedic surgery on both knee joints for knee flexion. This is a deformity that prevents the knee from straightening (also known as flexion contracture). Postoperatively, Leigh had both legs in plaster for six weeks. I can still remember carrying him around on my hip and trying to manage his bathing and toileting while keeping the plaster dry and clean.

It was impossible for us to take Leigh anywhere during this time because he could not fit into his current wheelchair; the cast would rub against the wheels, preventing the chair from moving freely. The loan wheelchair (pictured overleaf) could only be used as a means of support; it did not allow him to sit upright because

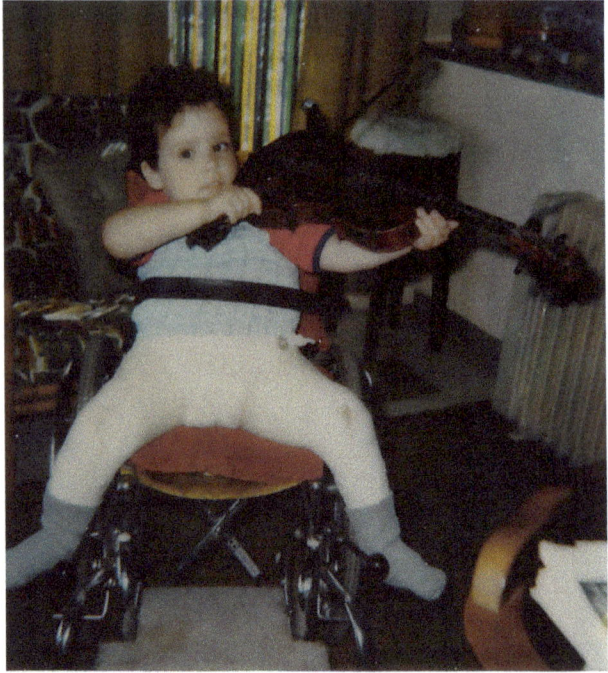

Pretending to play the violin (borrowed from maternal grandfather) with both legs in plaster after knee surgery.

of the angle of the cast. To solve this problem, I removed the loose seat cushions from our couch, exposing the rubber webbing, and used this as a 'support sling', enabling him to sit upright for meals and play. This was a simple but effective solution.

A large beanbag, popular in the '80s and '90s, was also helpful because it could be moulded into various shapes, but often the beans would shift under the weight of the cast and also make him sweat. We also found them very useful as a safe means of support when Leigh was young.

It was quite a challenging and exhausting time for both of us, but you carry on and think of ways to overcome obstacles as they arise. I had to think 'outside the box' many times!

The plaster cast was removed in October, but in the following days Leigh's right leg began to swell and a lump developed on the knee. X-rays were taken and he started a course of antibiotics. At home a few days later, a surgical pin pierced the skin where the lump had developed. It was back into hospital for a day or so to have the pin adjusted and continue the course of antibiotics.

★ ★ ★

The following year, more orthopaedic surgery was recommended – this time to Leigh's right hip. His left hip was mobile, but his right hip was fixed and in an adducted position (moving towards the body's midline). Surgeons acknowledged that Leigh was less likely to be a 'walker'. Their aim was to make him a good 'sitter' for wheelchair purposes, so a Girdlestone procedure was scheduled.

This surgery would release his right hip, giving him some pelvic movement and a better sitting position. The femoral head and neck are removed, but the head of the femur is not replaced. Instead, it is allowed to heal and develop its own fibrous scar tissue, creating a false joint. However, shortening of the leg is an inevitable outcome of this procedure.

Post-operative traction was then maintained for four weeks (three of which were at home) using a small, detachable pulley device and a bag of water as the counterweight. At night, the device was attached to the end of Leigh's bed; and during the day, it was attached to his wheelchair so that he could be kept mobile. Phillip drew on his engineering skills and designed and built a temporary seat–leg rest to accommodate the traction device. This consisted of a single piece of plywood shaped to fit on the seat of Leigh's wheelchair with an extension piece supporting his right leg straight and in an elevated position.

As Leigh's scoliosis progressed, the SB clinic doctors recommended spinal surgery in an effort to correct or halt the progress. In a letter dated 23 April 1992, the director of orthopaedics stated: 'The only solution I see for the progressive scoliosis is to do some form of surgical correction. Leigh is at an age where it may be possible to do "Zielke instrumentation" using screws and rods and correct the thoracolumbar curve.'

From my information in Leigh's extensive hospital files, a number of spinal instrumentation options were considered by different doctors. However, the 'Harrington rods' procedure was eventually decided on as the best choice for Leigh at the time.

> [The] **Harrington rod** is a surgical implant used to stretch the spine in order to correct abnormal curvature. The rod is attached to the spine with hooks inserted into the vertebra at the top of the curve and the vertebra at the bottom of the curve.
>
> The Harrington rod has a ratcheting mechanism that works to straighten the spinal curve and stabilize the spine. The vertebrae in between the hooks are then allowed to fuse.[5]

This surgery would be performed at a major hospital in the city of Melbourne by a team of medical professionals. After much deliberation and discussions with the surgeons and therapists, we felt this would be Leigh's best option at delaying, and hopefully correcting, some of the curvature, giving him a more comfortable sitting and/or standing position.

Leigh's rod surgery was performed on 16 March 1993 at 1.30 pm; he was eleven years old. I remember it vividly because the surgery

---

5   'Harrington rod definition' 2008, Spine-health, Veritas, <https://www.spine-health.com/glossary/harrington-rod>.

was abruptly halted and he was brought back out of theatre just half an hour later and placed on a ventilator in ICU. We were later informed that he had inadvertently been given breakfast by a nurse prior to the surgery, which caused him to vomit while under anaesthetic. This oversight could have had devastating consequences and I remember thinking, 'How could I put my boy through this ever again?' The surgery was postponed indefinitely so that Leigh could recover. We were left in a state of shock from this lapse of hospital protocol. How could something like this happen to a patient – a child – in their care?

Leigh spent a few days recovering in ICU while receiving antibiotics to clear his lungs of any infection. There was no mention of the person or persons involved and we never received an official apology from the hospital. We did, however, receive one apology from a visiting doctor who was indirectly involved with the surgery; maybe he was the self-appointed spokesperson for the others, I'm not sure, but he did express his concern at what had happened and offered 'his' apology!

I started to lose confidence in the hospital system. We had already gone through a number of previous orthopaedic surgeries with Leigh and encountered post-operative setbacks – whether or not to expose him to future surgery was an extremely difficult decision to consider. We were entrusting our son's wellbeing to these highly skilled professionals and these experiences had left us shaken.

Little did I know that this was just the beginning of much more heartache to come.

We agonised over putting Leigh through another attempt at the surgery. After much deliberation and reassurance from the medical team, it was decided this procedure was still his best option.

Leigh with a group from the Civil Aviation Authority's Rescue and Fire Fighting Service in Melbourne, Easter 1993.

I am not sure of the exact degree of Leigh's kyphoscoliosis at that time, but according the Cobb angle (a technique used to measure the degree of a curve on spinal X-ray), it might have been 40 degrees or more.

The surgery went ahead on 21 April and lasted more than eight hours, with two neurosurgeons and a team of medical personnel attending. Doctors advised us that everything had gone according to plan; we were glad that the surgery was over.

Following this marathon surgery, Leigh spent considerable time in hospital recovering. He needed blood transfusions and iron supplements to regain his strength. Leigh's happy infectious nature and familiarity with hospital protocols and staff enabled him to make friends very easily. During his many stays, he would often be an unwitting participant when special guests visited the hospitals. Leigh would meet people from all walks of life – from politicians during election time or the opening of a new hospital, to celebrities during the Easter appeals, and visiting Civil Aviation Authority personnel!

Leigh eventually returned home and we watched him closely, fearful of any repercussions after such an extensive procedure. I was very apprehensive about managing his care. How could I pick him up without hurting him? How could I bathe or place him on the toilet without causing any pain or discomfort?

Just six weeks after the surgery I noticed a wire protruding through the skin on his leg near his hip. As Leigh did not have any sensation below the waist, fortunately (for him) he could not feel the wire pushing out through his skin, which on all accounts would have been extremely painful. I was horrified. Not again!

Back in hospital, we were informed that Leigh's bones could not support the weight of the rods and that they had collapsed!

Revision surgery was scheduled for 1 June to extract the rods and wires. The doctors advised us that this would be extremely difficult and it was their hope not to create additional nerve

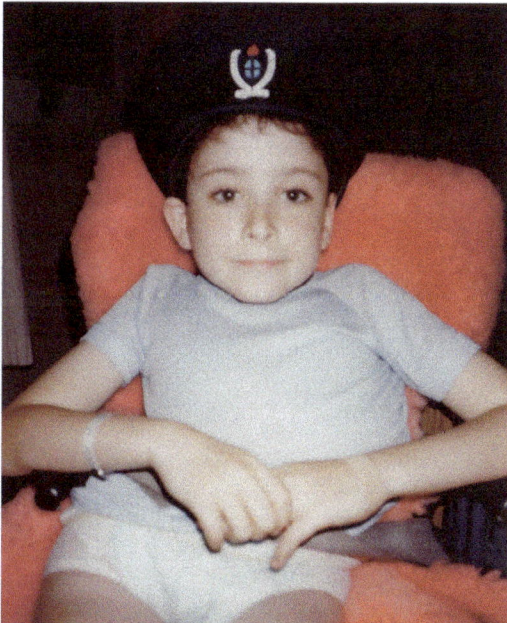

Putting on another brave face after the marathon rod surgery wearing a Rescue and Fire Fighting Service hat. Aged eleven.

damage. My poor boy, what had we done? We had entrusted the doctors to perform this radical surgical procedure, and now we were putting Leigh through more surgery to rectify the first! Was this a frequent outcome for such an invasive procedure?

The revised surgery seemed to last longer than the first, with more blood transfusions to follow. It left him weak and kept him away from home for some time. Still, we were amazed at just how resilient he was after each surgical procedure. He always had a smile for us when we visited him and was eager to talk about what was happening around him in the hospital and about the people he had met. Having spent considerable time in hospitals, unfortunately they had become very familiar places. He never complained; he just trusted his parents and accepted the doctors' treatments.

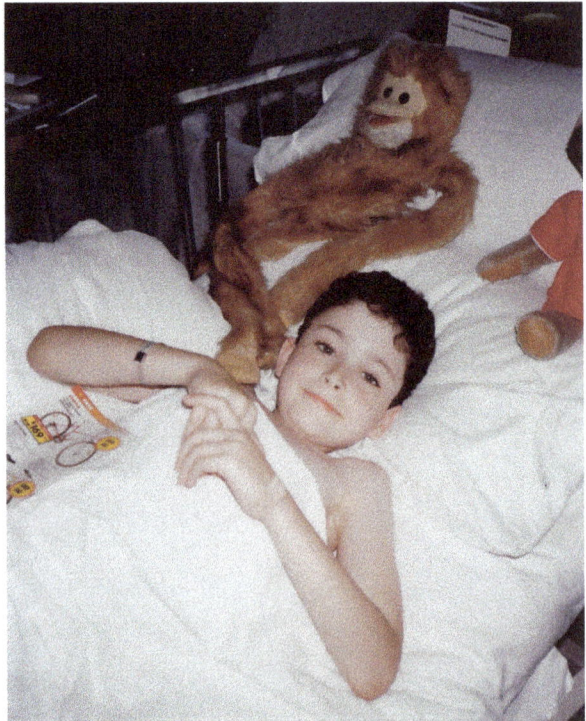

Leigh, age eleven, after
the rod removal surgery.

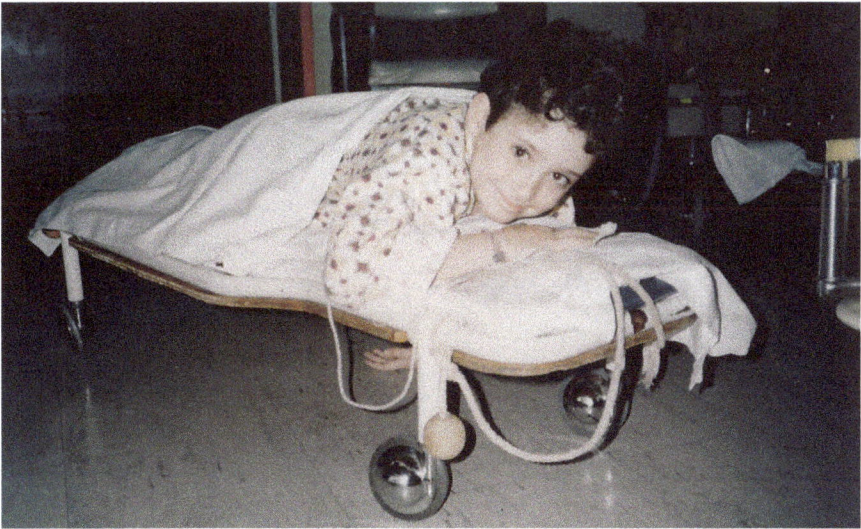

Using a low trolley board after back surgery to give him some relief from the hospital bed.

He would always be very optimistic and composed, as if it was all just another day. My amazing, beautiful boy!

However, our fears were later confirmed regarding additional nerve damage. According to a copy of a letter dated February 1994 (just ten months later) from a physician at the SB clinic to a social worker: 'Leigh has had a number of disastrous operations for his kyphoscoliosis, each of which has been associated with a perilous post-operative course causing considerable family stress. Leigh appears to have suffered some spinal cord damage as a result of these procedures.' He described Leigh's condition as 'a virtual complete paraplegia'.

★　★　★

A few years passed and we tried to avoid the hospitals and doctors, just getting on with normal family life. Leigh was thriving. However, we were advised at one of the SB clinics that he would still require some form of spinal surgery to help him sit upright, as the scoliosis was still a problem. With the horrors of the previous surgeries still fresh in our minds, we were reluctant to give our consent to yet another attempt.

The doctors reiterated their views and concerns, with one doctor stating, 'We have a window of opportunity to do the spinal surgery now while he's still young.' After much soul searching and a few sleepless nights, we gave the go-ahead and agreed for Leigh to have a spinal fusion surgery.

The procedure involved removing part of one of his lower ribs and using the bone from that to fuse the top part of his spine. The surgery went ahead without any complications; he now had a long scar across the bottom of his rib cage and an additional scar along the spine over the previous surgical scars. Leigh faced another long stay in hospital, away from home, but as always he never complained, he just accepted that this was his life and surgery was part of it.

★   ★   ★

Being in a wheelchair set Leigh apart from other children. I remember going shopping with him and sometimes a child would come over with a perplexed look on their face and ask him, 'Why are you in a wheelchair? Don't you miss walking?' Leigh would tell them, 'I was born this way. And no, I don't miss walking because I've never walked!' But it was the parents, with their open-mouthed stares, whispers and diverted eyes, who annoyed me. As an innocent child with a disability, Leigh had a strong sense of self so he would take all this in his stride.

CHAPTER 5

School Years, Sport and Beyond

With the assistance of teachers' aides, Leigh completed a modified mainstream school curriculum from kindergarten through to secondary college. At that time government schools offered little to cater to children with special needs, so we had

Leigh attending kindergarten in 1987, age five.

to push our case for Leigh to even be considered for enrolment, especially into the local secondary school.

During this period Phillip and I were shocked and amazed by the ignorance and closed-mindedness of some teachers towards children with special needs. Thankfully, our search ended when we met a forward-thinking headmaster of a local primary school who understood Leigh's requirements and our concerns, and was willing to assist. We were most grateful to him and the school community for supporting Leigh by organising a teacher's aide and providing infrastructure to accommodate his wheelchair, all before the start of a new school year.

With his happy disposition and eagerness to make friends, Leigh fitted in well at kindergarten and primary school, and the children were very receptive and obliging. One teacher's aide was a little overprotective of Leigh, as I later discovered. In class, she would write the majority of his school lessons because Leigh was very slow at writing and found it difficult to keep up. People close to Leigh were often eager to help whenever he looked a little lost and frustrated. She had unwittingly fallen for his charismatic ways and felt compelled to do everything for him!

I appreciated her efforts, but also recognised that Leigh was becoming lazy and not taking responsibility for his own work. After a quiet word with his teachers about my concerns, his lessons were slightly modified so that he could keep up with the other students. This made a huge difference to the way in which he approached his work.

It was important for Leigh to experience social activities with his friends. Going on school camps, joining the Scouts, and family day outings were such a thrill for Leigh – the look of excitement and anticipation on his face said it all. He loved being part of his peer group and doing 'normal things', just like all the other kids! District nursing services made it possible for Leigh to attend school camps. They would assist with his bedtime routine and check whether any wound dressings had become dislodged during the day's activities.

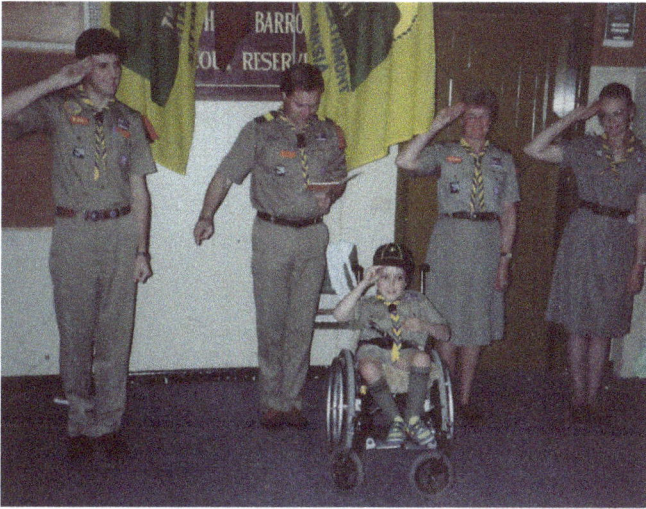

Leigh saluting during the Scouts pledge, aged six or seven.

We always wanted Leigh to experience new adventures and enjoy the fun things life had to offer, away from hospitals and medical appointments. However, family holidays and outings were often limited when he grew older due to his physical limitations and constant fear of falling.

He was very apprehensive and timid about venturing outside on his own and always sought reassurance from others, checking that the ground he was moving over was safe. As children, the boys loved the beach and playing in the sand; however, as Leigh grew older, carrying him or dragging a wheelchair across the sand or rough terrain was not an easy option.

Enjoying a family picnic with Leigh's maternal grandparents.

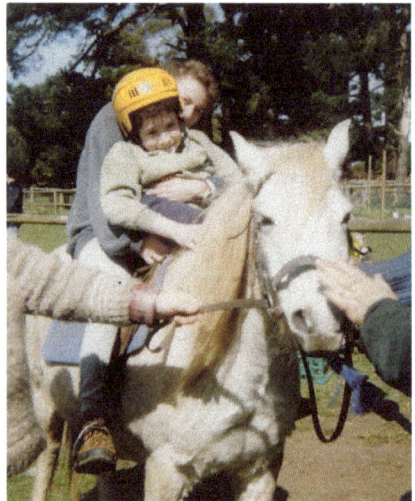

LEFT: Happy family memories! A camping holiday when the boys were seven and five. RIGHT: Leigh, about ten years old, nervously sitting on a horse during one of Interchange camps,

We discovered Interchange. Interchange Incorporated is a not-for-profit national organisation that supports agencies which offer social and recreational opportunities for people with disabilities and their carers. Leigh started attending their annual camping trips when he was about eight years old, and continued until he was thirteen. We felt reassured that he was in good hands and was well supported by enthusiastic volunteers and trained staff.

During his primary school days, Leigh also attended a wheelchair basketball venue, then called Sport and Recreation for Disabled Children (SRDC). Games were held every Saturday morning, which coincided with the monthly SB clinic, so we had to juggle the two to keep everyone happy. Children with various physical disabilities, but most with SB, participated in a friendly game of wheelchair basketball and other ball sports. This was a great way for Leigh to make new friends, build his upper-body strength and gain confidence using his wheelchair.

The organisation has since changed its name to Wheelchair Sports for Kids and continues to encourage children with disabilities to participate in a range of sporting activities.

At Christmas time, together with various charity organisations, the centre held great parties for the children. Sometimes television newsreaders or sporting celebrities make appearances and participated in a game or two using the wheelchairs. There were photo opportunities and gifts for the children, making it a great day for everyone. Medals and trophies were handed out to all the players for their efforts throughout the year. Leigh met a few major league footballers, basketball players, and some TV personalities along the way.

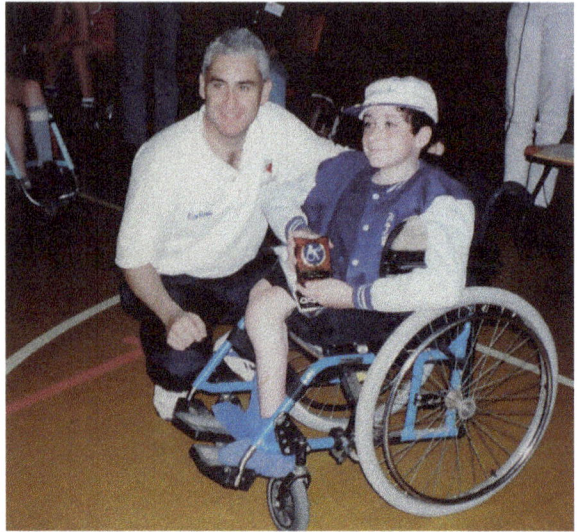

Aged thirteen at the
1995 SRDC Christmas
breakup meeting
weatherman Rob Gell.

When he was older, Leigh also played wheel rugby for a short time. For this, he needed a sports wheelchair – one that would allow him more agility and speed. He wanted to feel more involved and connected with his team mates, so having the right wheelchair was essential. However, being for recreational use only, it was considered a non-essential item; government funding for this type of equipment was limited, so we paid for it ourselves.

Most of Leigh's equipment (wheelchairs, shoes, callipers, etc.) was partially funded through the government Program of Aids for Disabled People scheme, now known as the State-wide Equipment Program (SWEP). There is a maximum subsidy guideline for funding on certain items and equipment – the parents or carer fund the remainder. Leigh's catheters were fully funded through the Continence Aids Assistance Scheme (CAAS), which changed to the Continence Aids Payment Scheme (CAPS) in 2010.

Leigh loved playing wheel rugby, which is a very physical sport and he became disheartened when he was forced to give it away

Basketball too tame for Leigh

By Peter Di Sisto

LEIGH McIver admits he had become somewhat "bored" playing wheelchair basketball and was keen to find a new interest.

The Bayswater North teenager recently discovered wheel rugby, a growing disabled sport which started in Canada in the late 1970s.

Wheel rugby, now in its 10th year in Australia, is played mainly by athletes with disabilities in all four limbs. It is said to be one of the world's fastest growing disabled sports.

There are four players per team, with the game played on a slightly modified basketball court using a volleyball. The aim is to move the ball into the opponents' half – a goal is scored when a player crosses the goal line while in possession of the ball. Players must also be aware of a number of positioning restrictions.

Leigh, who this past season helped the Spoke Busters to a second place finish in a competition played at Box Hill, is known for his "dogged" defensive play. He said he enjoys the competitive nature of the sport, which was originally known as a form of 'murder ball' in which anything goes.

"I'm very good at blocking other players, but I've also scored a couple of goals," he said. His colleagues believe he was integral to the team's recent success and he will, with time and experience,

"fill a role" in the Victorian state team.

Leigh told Post he wants to continue playing wheel rugby and would like to see more funding for disabled athletes to play sport at the elite level.

The Paralympics is the biggest stage for disabled sports, but it traditionally comes after the main event and is perhaps a victim of Olympics overdose. Some suggest that the Paralympics would be better as an appetiser.

Leigh McIver of Bayswater North plays what is reputedly the fastest growing wheelchair sport in the world. Unfortunately Leigh and fellow disabled athletes may miss out on the chance to perform at the elite level.

Leigh interviewed here for the *Knox Post* (no longer in circulation) on 17 June 1998, age sixteen, proudly showing some of his basketball medals.

due to the scoliosis causing discomfort and difficulties with transfers.

★   ★   ★

Secondary school presented new challenges for Leigh; he now had to share his aide with other students with special needs.

The first year was very daunting for him; he had to organise his own workload and take responsibility for himself. He found this extremely difficult and as he struggled to keep up with the normal school curriculum, he became withdrawn and lost his happy disposition.

We organised a meeting with Leigh's teachers to share our thoughts on his strengths and weaknesses, and how we could all work together to make Leigh's school life a little easier. I offered my insight on what he struggled with and what he excelled at academically.

Leigh still contended with poor eye–hand coordination (a perceptual motor skill). He had trouble remembering what was said or seen (a short-term memory skill) and found organising or preparing himself difficult. He also struggled to make decisions on his own, and problem solving was a challenge.

However, one of Leigh's strengths was his mathematical skills. He could quickly calculate numerical problems in his head and on occasion would correct nurses on their calculation of his medication dosage, which was a little disconcerting for me!

The teachers were very responsive to our discussion and Leigh's lessons were again modified accordingly. We noticed a huge change for the better in his attitude towards school; he was completing set tasks and his schoolwork improved considerably. He enjoyed getting up in the morning, going to school and being part of the school community. He especially enjoyed drama classes, which gave him a chance to dress up, escape from reality and become someone else for a while. Leigh just wanted to be involved with whatever was going on at school and to be accepted as an equal. This was his wish throughout his life; to just fit in!

In drama class, he met Chris Hemsworth, who was also a student at the time – he might even have begun his acting career there! After leaving school, Leigh followed Chris's career religiously and watched all his movies many times over, telling anyone who was interested that he went to school with 'Thor'!

★　★　★

The time came when we needed to update our home to suit Leigh's and our requirements. In our double-storey house, which we had purchased one year prior to Leigh's birth, all the bedrooms and the main bathroom were upstairs. Downstairs, there was a small

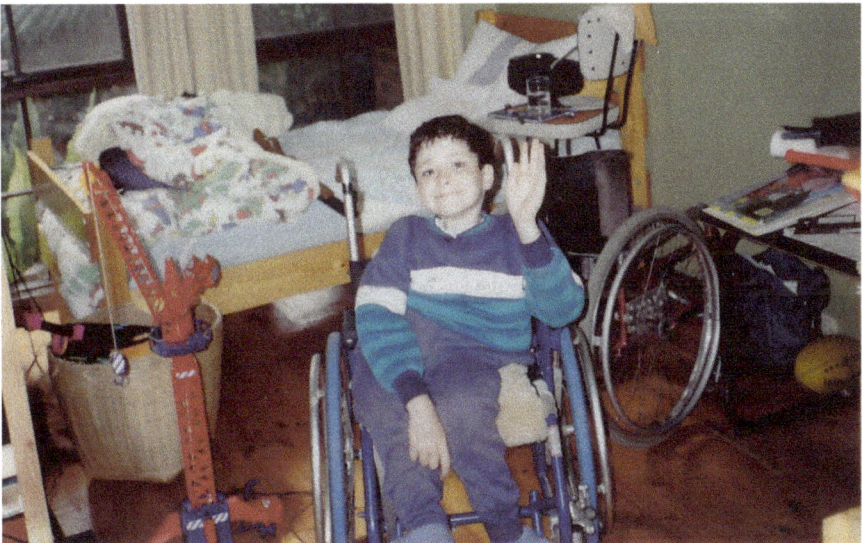

Happy to be downstairs in his converted bedroom previously a study. Aged around ten years.

powder room with a hand basin and toilet, as well as a small study. Leigh was happy for the study to be converted into his bedroom, but we still had major problems with bathroom arrangements. We decided to extend the powder room out into the adjacent laundry to include a large shower area that would accommodate a commode chair, mobile hoist, support rails, a low toilet and a vanity basin, all contained in the one area. Our current routine was for me to carry Leigh upstairs for bathing. (He weighed about 40 kilos.) When he was younger he would try to pull himself up the stairs, one step at a time, in an effort to save me from lifting him, but this proved too difficult for him as he got older and heavier.

We looked at installing a lift, but through researching we dis-covered that the angle of the staircase was too sharp and the cost of installing a new stairwell and lift was far beyond our means.

It was recommended through the SB clinic that we submit an application to SWEP to assist with the bathroom renovation. The application was approved, but only funded 25 per cent of the renovation; Make a Difference, a charity organisation, generously assisted with donations that covered 60 per cent of the works; and we funded the remaining 15 per cent.

It wasn't until 1988, when Leigh was about sixteen, that the renovations were finally completed. The funding was an enormous help to our family and made a considerable difference to Leigh's toileting and bathing routine. We could now move around freely in the bathroom and use his equipment with ease.

⋆   ⋆   ⋆

Following secondary school, I enrolled Leigh at Swinburne TAFE in the outer suburbs of Melbourne, where he completed a

Studying at Swinburne TAFE in 2004, age twenty-two. He was going through a 'moustache phase' at the time, emulating his father.

Certificate I in Work Education. Going to TAFE was another huge endeavour for him – this time there was no teacher's aide to assist or organise his workload. However, I felt he needed to make the transition from school into the workforce; life was always going to be a challenge.

The TAFE course, however, was specifically designed for students who had difficulties in the mainstream educational system, and provided support and assistance while preparing them for employment and/or further education. It was a solid stepping stone for Leigh as he transitioned into the workforce, building his confidence through accomplishing something on his own – receiving a certificate on completion was a bonus.

We extended the course for two years, giving Leigh ample time to complete all the set tasks; it also gave him time to think about what he wanted to do next in his life.

During these two years at TAFE, Leigh made some genuine and long-lasting friendships. One friend in particular was Simon, who he later met up with again when he started work at Nadrasca.

★   ★   ★

I started researching suitable avenues of employment for Leigh; being a productive member of society was important to him. He modelled his work ethics on those of his parents – both Phillip and I always held long-term employment – and this showed later in Leigh's attitude towards his work commitments. But finding suitable employment was not going to be easy. Discrimination, whether blatant or disguised, was a major barrier. In one instance, Leigh was informed that he could not be offered employment due to the risk of other employees falling over his wheelchair as their office space was limited.

However, I came across a company called Nadrasca Industries, a not-for-profit supported employment service in the eastern suburbs

Leigh and Simon at a Nadrasca Christmas function in either 2014 or 2015.

of Melbourne. The parent company was set up in 1967 and provides a range of services (including training, employment and accommodation) for people with a disability. I felt they could offer Leigh innovative employment and training in a safe, non-judgemental environment. He could develop new skills and make some friends along the way. I wasn't sure what type of work he could handle, either physically or emotionally, but I knew he needed to be out in the workforce and not home alone.

A meeting was set up with their recruitment officer to discuss employment possibilities, and an initial tour of the factory was arranged. Leigh was a little overwhelmed by the size of the warehouse and felt apprehensive about the duties he would be undertaking, but with our encouragement, he was eager to start work; excited at the prospect of starting a new phase in his life and making new friends.

This was a huge step for him and for us, with many new experiences ahead to learn from and cope with. Leigh sometimes struggled to keep up the pace of going to work each day – getting up early, dressing and maintaining his overall health – but he always enjoyed the sense of accomplishment and being part of the team.

Leigh commenced work at Nadrasca in 2006 and he was there until his passing in October 2016. Although he was only one of two workers in a wheelchair at that time, he was never excluded from any of the activities. Initially, he worked a full five-day week, from 8.30 am to 4.30 pm, but he was struggling to maintain this workload, so his working week was reduced to four days.

Leigh worked for a minimum wage. For more than five years I drove him to and from work, lifting him and the wheelchair in and out of the car, until part-funding for maxi cab fares became available. The cost of fares was always much higher than his entire take-home pay, even with his taxi discount card (entitling him to 50% off the standard fare), so additional funding was vital. This came from a Linkages Package paid through Department of Human Services (DHS), which provides top-up funding for people with complex care needs that cannot be fully met by standard Home and Community Care services. Funds were allocated by his service provider and, in this instance, covered cab fare vouchers and incontinence products.

Leigh's working week would vary from packing chocolates or dairy products one day to weighing tools the next. He also occasionally worked in the office processing data on the computer, which he enjoyed. Sometimes he had interesting stories to tell, but he was always very tired on his return home and often didn't have a lot to say. But I knew he was satisfied with what he had achieved and we were very proud of his accomplishments.

Because of all the orthopaedic surgery, Leigh's height was compromised; his potential height would have been about 182 centimetres (six feet). His short stature made him look much younger than his years, which sometimes made him feel uncomfortable when meeting people for the first time. They would often mistake him for a child and sometimes talk down to him, which would infuriate him and me. If I noticed this during the conversation, I would quickly point out that Leigh was employed and working, which would draw their attention to his age. This often helped alleviate embarrassment for both parties.

Initially, Leigh used a manual wheelchair at work and it was sometimes difficult for him to reach certain table heights to complete particular jobs. However, Nadrasca generously provided

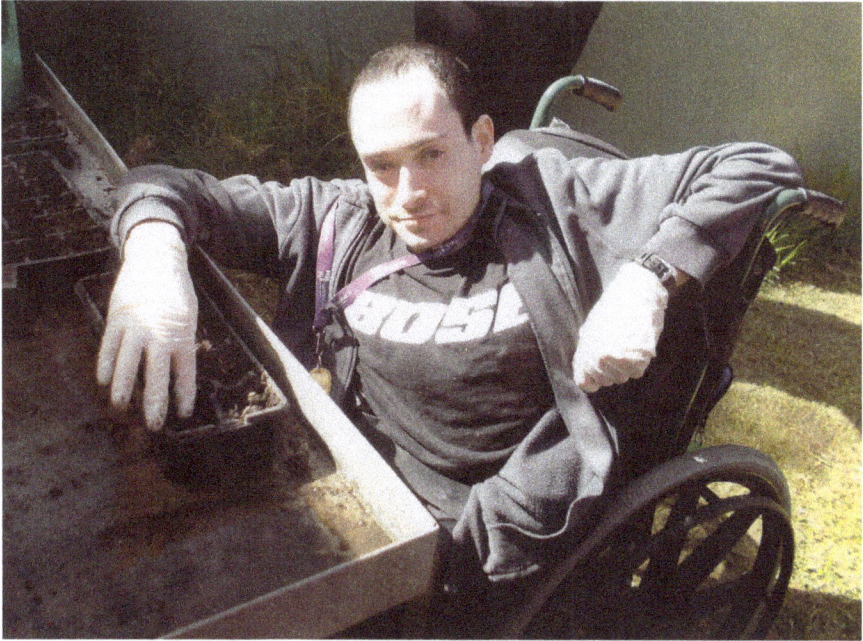

Planting seedlings at Nadrasca's farm.

a new electric wheelchair that gave him more flexibility to fulfil work commitments.

Leigh was very excited about receiving his first (and only) electric wheelchair. It gave him a sense of importance and belonging. He never liked to be called 'special', so I would never use this word when referring to him, but he certainly did feel 'special' because he could now raise himself and work at any table height. He could also tilt the chair back to get some relief from sitting upright all day. But the best part of having an electric wheelchair was that he could now keep up with his friends and go fast! He delighted in telling me how he would sometimes speed around the factory floor and corridors when no one was looking. This explained the occasional bruising to his arms and elbows – the result of misjudging his speed and cutting the corners too sharply!

CHAPTER 6

Family Changes

Life for our family was going great; everyone was well and working. At twenty-six, Leigh had no more surgeries scheduled – he was in good health and happy.

But tragedy struck on the night of Friday, 16 May 2008. Phillip and his younger brother Ian, together with Jason and Shanta (his partner at the time), were attending a night-time football match when he suddenly collapsed. I was contacted at home by Shanta who told me that he had supposedly fainted. Unfortunately, Jason witnessed Phillip's collapse and the furious attempts of bystanders as they tried to help him. An off-duty doctor used a portable defibrillator to try to restart his heart. I vividly remember hearing the frantic cries of Jason and others in the background while I listened on the phone, telling Phillip to breathe. He was taken by ambulance to a major hospital in Melbourne, where he remained unconscious.

I told Leigh that I had to go to the hospital because his father was unwell and left him in bed, watching the television.

When I arrived at the hospital's emergency ward, Phillip was still unconscious. Within a few hours doctors advised us that they had done all they could. Phillip had never regained consciousness and died a few hours after being admitted. We were all in a state of shock.

When Jason and I returned home it was late and Leigh was already asleep. I didn't have the heart to wake him then to tell him about his father's passing. Jason and I told him the following morning, which was extremely difficult for all of us.

★   ★   ★

Phillip had a Diploma in Mechanical Engineering and was very committed to his work. He spent long days at work, leaving home at seven in the morning and sometimes not getting home until seven or eight at night.

A workaholic, he rarely took sick leave or holidays and, when he did, would constantly worry about work. I often told him to slow down and rest, but he would tell me that all the long work hours were to make a better future for our family. I often wondered if this was his way of coping with Leigh's disability and his own health issues.

In 1992, Phillip was having occasional pain or tightness in his chest. He put this down to heartburn from eating rushed meals. We had had our fill of doctors and hospitals and, when you are young, you think you are invincible and so he dismissed it. One day, he came home unusually early, complaining that the pain in his chest was more severe. I immediately drove him to the local doctor's surgery where we had to wait to be seen by the doctor on duty, even though Phillip was still suffering severe chest pains. He was eventually seen by a GP who advised him that he was probably suffering from 'stress' or having a 'panic attack' and prescribed antidepressants. She then advised him to go home, rest and take things easy.

Back home, the pain continued to escalate, so out of fear and frustration I drove Phillip to the local hospital Emergency Department where we were later advised that he had actually suffered a heart attack! We were both shocked and angry that this had not been diagnosed by the GP earlier. Phillip was only forty-one when he had his first heart attack; Jason was twelve and Leigh was ten.

Phillip now had angina and was on medication to help keep it under control, which meant that he could no longer do any of the heavy lifting associated with Leigh's care, and this concerned him greatly. Tests revealed that he had a number of blocked arteries and a subsequent heart attack was highly likely, but he chose not to have a stent or bypass surgery, instead opting for a healthier lifestyle: exercise, special diet and alternative therapies. Stent surgery was not as advanced as it is today; I think he was concerned that the procedure may not be successful and that it would have to be redone over time.

After the heart attack, Phillip became depressed; he would constantly apologise to me for not being able to help more. He hid his depression well from family and friends, but despite my constant requests for him to seek professional help he instead chose to submerge himself in his work.

However, despite lifestyle changes and trialling complementary therapies, including chelation therapy (intravenous infusion of substances intended to remove calcium from hardened arteries), Phillip's second heart attack came without warning, as medical personnel had predicted.

Phillip passed away in 2008; he was only fifty-seven. There was a history of heart disease in the family, with his father passing from a heart attack and his mother from a cardiac aneurysm, both in their mid-fifties.

This was an extremely difficult time for us. I lost my loving husband and best friend of thirty-two years and our sons lost their wonderful father. Jason was twenty-eight and Leigh twenty-six, but the brotherly bond established during their childhood continued to grow after Phillip's passing. Through their love, support and caring nature they both became my strength to carry on.

Some time later, while reluctantly sifting through Phillip's paperwork at home, I came across an exercise on goal setting that he had completed while attending one of many work seminars and conferences:

Sitting on a Moonbeam

You are sitting on a moonbeam and looking down on yourself ten years from now. You see the life you are living, the people who surround you, and the way you fill your days.

Q: How would you describe yourself?
A: I am satisfied with what I have achieved.

Q: What have you achieved?
A: A secure family relationship and respect from friends and peers.

Q: Who are the most important people in your life?
A: My wife and family.

Q: How are you spending your time?

A: The simplest pleasures.

Q: What are your most pressing concerns or worries in your life right now?

A: Building a positive working environment regardless of who else enjoys the journey!

When a loved one is taken from you suddenly, every piece of the life they left behind is extremely important – this questionnaire, as small as it was, is very precious to me. I must admit I was taken aback when I first read it and have re-read it many times since, trying to interpret Phillip's feelings. I can sense his anxiety and helplessness at not being able to help more with Leigh's care. He also carried a fear that his work colleagues would pick up on his health issues and somehow think less of him, and job security was very important. I interpreted his last answer as feeling anxious about trying to establish his career as a production manager without compromising family life.

★   ★   ★

We all dealt with Phillip's death in our own way.

I became reclusive, not eating properly, not sleeping and only leaving the house when I needed to buy food and necessities for the boys. About a month later I left my long-term employment to rethink my future and the future of our boys, and to consider what direction to take in my life. Jason and Leigh were, and are, everything to me. Without them, I do not know how I would have coped during that dark time.

Jason is my rock. He, too, is a quiet and caring son, but he often keeps his feelings hidden. He was reluctant to talk about his father's

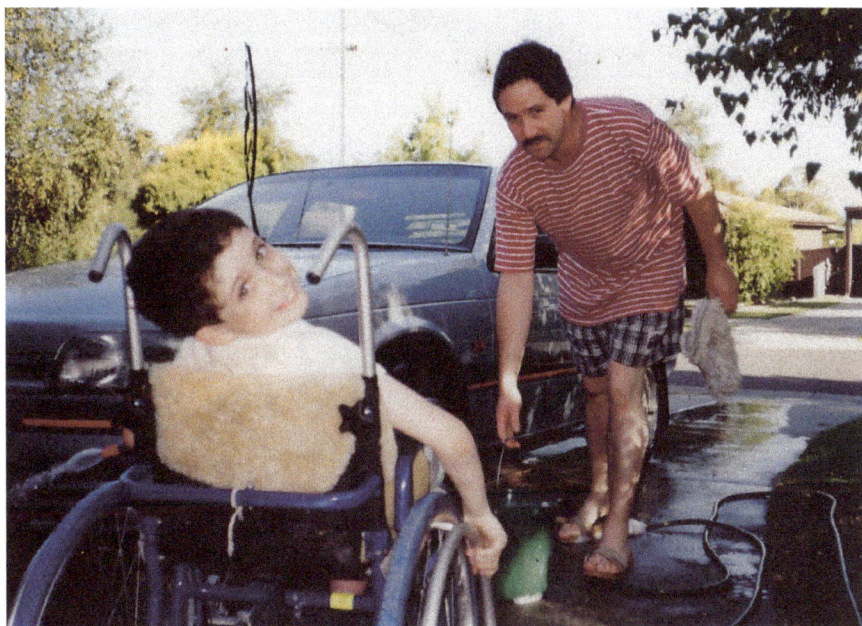

Leigh loved helping his father whenever possible, especially washing the family car – which was usually a Sunday afternoon tradition – although it usually ended up in a water fight! Leigh would have been about nine or ten.

death and it was some time before he was able to divulge a few of the details of that tragic night. However, he was always there to help with any jobs around the house and to listen whenever I needed to talk. He always offered to help with Leigh's care, but I felt it just wasn't right for him to be involved with his brother's bowel or wound care, and Leigh felt the same. Jason was always on hand to fix a flat tyre or tighten a bolt on Leigh's wheelchair. He encouraged Leigh to try different activities – target shooting was a particular favourite. Together they flew model aeroplanes, drones and kites, and had a common interest in computer games and puzzles. Nothing was too much effort for Jason when it came to helping Leigh follow his interests and achieve his goals.

Leigh hid his grief well from his friends at work. But at home I would make a point of talking about happier times with his father – this would bring a smile to his face. I made sure we all mentioned Phillip's name and reminisced about some of the funny things he would do: falling asleep and snoring while watching TV; sleeping at his computer and falling off the chair; how he loved peanut butter and honey sandwiches, and his obsession over everything to do with car racing and football. It was good to hear the boys laugh and smile while remembering their father.

Relatives on both sides of our family were hesitant to mention Phillip's name during the early years of his passing. When a loved one dies, family and friends are often reluctant to mention their name around those left behind. Perhaps they think this will only cause more pain from remembering happier times – I'm not sure.

For me, this had the opposite effect – not mentioning Phillip's name only added to the stress of the loss by not acknowledging, remembering and celebrating his life ... his existence!

Leigh became very protective of his family and concerned for my welfare; he would constantly ask if I was okay. It was sometimes difficult to keep my poker face on around him because he was very sensitive and quick to read my face and body language. He seemed to sense when I was not having a good day. He would often hold my hand while we travelled in the car, just to show me that he was there and understood how I was feeling. He was a great source of comfort to me.

As months and years passed, the reality of Phillip's sudden death and the uncertainty of our future slowly began to sink in. I wanted to reach out to other women who had lost a partner and find comfort in our shared stories. I researched local support groups and it soon became clear that there was no suitable group for younger widows in my area. After some soul searching and encouragement from my boys, I decided to start one.

I had no idea how to go about this and didn't feel confident enough to speak to strangers about my ideas. I decided to draft a flyer regarding the need for a support group for younger widows and widowers. I found it difficult to refer to myself as a 'widow'. (Even now I still think of myself as being married rather than as a widow, and I found this to be a common feeling among the members.) However, the group is called 'The Widows and Widowers Support Group'.

I emailed the flyer to a number of councils in the surrounding areas. To my surprise, I received favourable feedback from a number of councils with offers to advertise the group free of charge in their local newsletters. The idea seemed to be very popular, so I eventually approached Maroondah City Council for a venue. The rest is history.

The group was officially established in 2009 in Croydon, Victoria. In the early days we met once a month with only a few people attending. Eventually the group grew to fifteen or more people of varying ages. I also organised guest speakers to cover a variety of subjects, including a guided meditation session with a Buddhist monk and the uplifting words of a motivational speaker. These talks helped to focus and enlighten the mind and were well received. I made some good friends during my time with the group and we still keep in touch to this day.

The group is now run by the Australian Centre for Grief and Bereavement and still meets once a month. (Contact details can be found at the end of this book.)

CHAPTER 7

Growing Older, Rising Health Issues

During the years following Phillip's passing, Leigh – now in his late twenties – started to suffer various health problems. He had a number of episodes of severe, prolonged gastroenteritis. He was dehydrated and had to be hospitalised for more than a week in order to be rehydrated and have tests to determine the underlying cause.

These episodes were horrific due to his lack of bowel control and the inability to sense when he needed to go. He weighed approximately 55 kilos, and lifting him quickly from his bed and onto the toilet or commode chair was an effort. We did have a mobile hoist, but it was not always possible or practical to use it in these situations.

He had pneumonia a couple of times, necessitating hospitalisation, and twice he had cellulitis (a potentially serious bacterial infection of the inner layer of skin) in his legs, each occurrence requiring a two-week hospital stay for intravenous antibiotics.

Leigh's energy levels started to drop and he developed an occasional cough, which became more noticeable toward the end of the day, at night, and whenever he was tired.

He would slowly recover after each illness and be eager to get back to work. But he was not sleeping well, was run-down and often tired, especially at the end of the day. I could not put my finger on what was going on with him, but I knew something wasn't right.

In 2012 Leigh, now aged thirty, became disorientated after getting out of bed one the morning: he was confused, shaking, short of breath and had trouble talking. He could not indicate to me how he was feeling, and I knew it was not a seizure from the symptoms, so I called an ambulance. The paramedics advised me that his heart rate was dangerously fast (190–200 BPM). They administered oxygen, transferred him onto a stretcher, and rushed him into the waiting ambulance. I can still remember watching them pull away from the curb and the sirens blaring as they left our street. I stood frozen in disbelief. What had just happened? I followed the ambulance in a daze, wondering what was going on with my boy.

Leigh had chest X-rays to check for pneumonia or any heart condition and a head CT scan to rule out any shunt blockages. He had numerous blood tests, which revealed high levels of carbon dioxide (CO_2), a condition known as hypercapnia (or hypercarbia). Doctors explained that, when functioning normally, the body uses up the oxygen in the blood and the waste product – the CO_2 – is exhaled through the lungs. Leigh's tests clearly indicated that his lungs were not functioning well. The fact that Leigh might one day suffer from hypercapnia had never been explained to me, so this diagnosis came as a huge shock.

The realisation that Leigh's scoliosis had now begun to compromise his breathing concerned me greatly.

After the diagnosis I discovered through my own research that high levels of CO_2 are extremely dangerous and can lead to coma or even death. Symptoms include headaches, lethargy, drowsiness and confusion – all of which Leigh had experienced at home prior to me calling the ambulance. Why hadn't I been warned earlier, when we were exploring surgical options for the scoliosis, that Leigh might develop this condition? Why hadn't I been advised to monitor him for this potentially life-threatening condition?

★   ★   ★

While reading through my own extensive hospital files on Leigh for this biography, I came across two letters. One letter, dated 4 May 2000, was attached behind an *earlier* letter, dated 5 February 2000.

At this time, Leigh was eighteen and no longer attending the SB clinic, which is significant because the February letter was from an SB clinic doctor who was concerned enough to write to a paediatric respiratory physician, stating that he suspected Leigh had a diminished respiratory reserve and asking for Leigh to be seen within the next two to four weeks for a respiratory evaluation.

Leigh was evaluated and the findings were detailed in a letter to his GP (the May letter): reduced air entry over the right hemithorax (side of the chest) and very poor pulmonary function. He also stated that the Harrington rod surgery had been unsuccessful and that further spinal surgery should be approached with caution. Most importantly, he went on to recommend a sleep study *as soon as possible* to assess whether Leigh was experiencing hypoxia (insufficient oxygen reaching body tissue) and to ensure that he was not hypoventilating (breathing at an abnormally slow rate). Both of these conditions would result in an increased amount of CO_2 in the blood.

Sadly the GP never actioned this letter. In hindsight, if a sleep study had been carried out as recommended and it were to have revealed that Leigh was experiencing either hypoxia or hypoxaemia (an oxygen deficiency in arterial blood), Leigh could have been given a breathing device to use at night and we would have at least become aware of any respiratory problems, such as hypercapnia.

★ ★ ★

Leigh was then transferred to a respiratory support service unit at another hospital. He commenced treatment using a variable positive airway pressure (VPAP) machine. This is an auto-adjusting, bi-level breathing device that provides two levels of pressure, matching natural inhalation and exhalation rhythms. It can also be used to treat sleep apnoea and other sleep disorders.

After a sleep study session, adjustments were made to the VPAP machine settings and Leigh quickly recovered. He came home with this machine and an oxygen concentrator, which delivers oxygen into the VPAP. Two separate oxygen tanks were subsequently delivered to the house. These could be attached to the back of the wheelchair for when Leigh was mobile or away from home. He would only use the oxygen during the day if he felt tired or out of breath. As Leigh slowly improved, he only required the oxygen at night. Once his CO_2 levels had improved, the oxygen ceased and only the VPAP unit was used during the night.

Leigh had to adjust to sleeping with a full facemask and a machine pushing air into his lungs at set intervals. Jason and I also had to adjust to sleeping with the cacophony of sounds emitting from Leigh's bedroom every night: the concentrator machine that sounded like a puffing steam train with its reverberating hum and constant gushes of air; the air mattress pump vibrating on the floorboards under his bed; and the occasional shrill as air leaked from the facemask seal whenever it wasn't properly fitted.

We certainly had a few sleepless nights and resorted to putting layers of foam on the floor under the air mattress pump and concentrator to reduce the vibration and noise level. In time, we also became familiar with the sounds, and Leigh learned to adjust his facemask.

In the following weeks, Leigh slept well using his VPAP machine. I started to see a huge improvement in his health and overall wellbeing. He was more alert and his energy levels had improved. He had that 'sparkle' back in his beautiful eyes; Leigh was getting back to his old self and enjoying life.

Leigh was monitored through a VPAP outpatient clinic on a monthly basis. His CO_2 levels would be checked and the VPAP machine settings would be adjusted when necessary. Taking blood for this test was extremely painful for him. Medically termed a venipuncture blood sample, it is the collection of blood from a vein on the inside of the elbow or the back of the hand. Leigh was an old pro at handling normal injections, but he'd wince during this procedure.

Some time later, Leigh was well enough to return to work with an oxygen tank attached to his wheelchair. Nadrasca was very supportive and management set up safety procedures and provided training for their staff on how to use the oxygen tank.

★   ★   ★

Some years later, while attending to Leigh's bowel care, I noticed a small amount of blood appearing after his bowel movements.

When this became more pronounced, I organised an appointment for him to be seen at a gastroenterology clinic through the local hospital. However, before the appointment date Leigh became unwell again and was admitted into hospital for tests. His iron count was extremely low so he was given three blood transfusions. His health quickly improved and, on discharge, he was advised to make another gastroenterology appointment, which he did.

Leigh attended the scheduled appointment a month later and a dietary iron supplement was prescribed. He was also scheduled for a colonoscopy, but considering his past respiratory problems, he was first referred to an anaesthesiologist to determine if he could undergo the light anaesthetic.

The doctors concluded that the procedure would be too risky and that having it done *without* anaesthesia would cause significant distress. In addition, Leigh's body shape would also make the colonoscopy very difficult.

Some weeks later we were back at the gastroenterology clinic to find out what other options were available.

The doctor briefly touched on other non-invasive screening methods including an MRI or CT scan. A follow-up appointment was scheduled for six months time, but before this Leigh became unwell yet again with high levels of CO_2 and breathing problems.

CHAPTER 8

New and Ongoing Challenges

As Leigh's health issues increased, I watched my beautiful, bubbly son sink into a deep depression. Nothing can prepare you for this. You are completely helpless, unable to offer comfort or respite.

★　★　★

Leigh had been a delight to raise as a child and care for as an adult, with his easygoing, quiet, calm nature and endless patience. He would always tell me, 'Don't worry, Mum, I'm OK.'

He thought going to hospital, attending clinics, having scans and surgeries and taking lots of medication were all part of a 'normal' life. In his eyes, it was just the way it was. I often worried about how he was going to cope when he realised that his life *was* different. How could I prepare him for this? Would it be a gradual connection, or would something – or someone – trigger doubts about who he was and how different his life was?

★　★　★

As a child, after coming back from a long stay in hospital, Leigh would often have nightmares and wake up crying. Although these night terrors eventually diminished, he still carried unsettling memories of hospitals and surgeries into adulthood. We would often talk about those times, and I would be quick to reassure him that the past was the past and to look forward to the future!

Once, Leigh woke up crying in the middle of the night; he told me he'd heard people talking about him in the other room, so I checked the other rooms to appease him. This behaviour continued to get worse and he started telling me that people at work hated him and were saying derogatory things behind his back. It was a daily struggle for him to go to work and this concerned me greatly, as it was completely out of character. I spoke with his managers and colleagues; they had also noticed a change in his behaviour and were eager to assist in any way they could.

I sought the help of a psychologist to help Leigh speak openly about what was troubling him. Leigh soon felt that these sessions were not helping and was reluctant to continue. I spoke with the psychologist about my concerns and he agreed that Leigh would benefit more from seeing a psychiatrist who could prescribe suitable medication for his anxiety and depression.

While I searched for a psychiatrist experienced in treating patients with special needs, Leigh became increasingly worse, having episodes of abnormal thinking and distorted perception of things or situations. I had never encountered this behaviour in him and became increasingly concerned for his welfare. I was at a loss as to how to respond or assist him. Leigh eventually stopped talking altogether and refused to eat or drink. I was totally puzzled and fearful for his wellbeing, and was forced to take him to hospital again in case he became dehydrated or worse.

He was admitted into a public hospital and assessed by various doctors who suggested he spend time in the hospital's Inpatient Psychiatric Unit (IPU), where he would receive counselling and medication to help with his symptoms. He was prescribed a course of antidepressants and referred to a psychiatrist outside the hospital for continued treatment. Leigh spent two weeks in the IPU, receiving medication and counselling, and apart from all the usual issues with his personal care needs, he slowly became well enough to come home.

Leigh then received scheduled visits at home from the Crisis Assessment and Treatment Team (CATT) to monitor his progress. This is a multidisciplinary team of mental health professionals that provides assessment and intensive treatment to people who are in crisis or experiencing an acute phase of mental illness. These dedicated professionals were an integral part of Leigh's successful recovery; I appreciated their care and support during this difficult phase.

Leigh started his sessions with the psychiatrist outside the hospital on a fortnightly basis. With appropriate medication and counselling, his mental clarity slowly improved. He was talking openly again and eating regular meals, getting back to his old self. This was a huge relief for Jason and me, but it left me wondering what had caused Leigh to become so unwell so quickly and whether there was any chance of him relapsing.

The doctor advised me that sometimes people with a brain injury – or in Leigh's case, 'shunts' – may develop neurological problems!

I came to accept Leigh's depression would be long-term and that he would have to continue taking medication to stay well.

This was a small price to pay for his much-improved state of mind. Mental health was a completely new area of learning for me and another hurdle for our small family to overcome.

I am sure the sudden passing of Leigh's father was a major contributory factor that triggered these episodes and I am grateful to the doctors in IPU who were quick to assess Leigh's condition and get him started on the correct medication and treatment.

Around the same time, Leigh also lost a work colleague and good friend, Robbie Wright, who was tragically murdered. Two people (both with disabilities) were charged with his murder, having pushed him off a second-storey balcony to his death. As Robbie was hearing impaired, he was unaware of their presence and, taken by surprise he did not defend himself. I believed Leigh would be distraught at this news, but he did not show any emotion upon receiving it, which I found very disconcerting. The psychiatrist spoke to Leigh about this and helped him to process the situation.

After some weeks, Leigh was able to go back to work. With encouragement from his friends and family, he made steps toward a good recovery. I did, however, keep a close watch on him. He continued the sessions with the psychiatrist on a monthly basis, which gradually decreased to six-monthly sessions.

If you or someone you are caring for have any mental health issues, please seek professional help – it is so readily available!

★   ★   ★

Leigh was also dealing with chronic (persistent or constantly recurring) pressure ulcers on his back (where his rib cage would rub against any surface) and right hip. He had very sensitive skin that easily ulcerated if any surface rubbed or pressed against it, such as seating systems that he had outgrown. This was largely due to poor circulation in areas where he had little or no sensation. This lack of sensation started just above his waistline and affected all the lower parts of his body. While helping him to dress or shower I would check his skin for reddened patches or grazes in order to address them quickly before they developed into chronic or persistent ulcers.

As the curve in Leigh's spine became more pronounced, when seated his right hip would connect with, and rest on, his lower rib. Consequently, the ulcer on this hip was the most difficult to treat and dress because the area was so restricted; in addition, the heat from his body made the dressings continually slide off.

Leigh desperately needed a new specialised seating system to help keep him as upright as possible and prevent these chronic ulcers, which could take months or even years to heal.

During his hospital admissions, whether from poor communication during staff handover, a shortage of wound supplies, or lack of wound care training (or all the above), Leigh's wound care needs were often not appropriately addressed and new ulcers would develop. I would always make a point of telling the doctors and nurses about his ulcers, hoping that proper care would be taken to prevent new ones occurring. At these times, his poor health would also exacerbate existing ulcers, and infections would occur.

Upon my advice, Leigh would be placed on an air mattress but on many occasions the mattress would be faulty, with some of the air cells not inflating, hence providing little or no pressure relief and subsequently causing more skin trauma.

In addition, a 'pinky' absorbent cloth bed mat would often be placed on top of the air mattress. This mat would rub against his skin, defeating the purpose of the air mattress. I would often comment on this practice only to be told, 'This is what we do here – it's easier for us to use the pinky mat to slide him up the bed.' I was astounded! Leigh's legs were often pressed together whenever he lay in bed in the same position for long periods of time. This would make his legs sweat, resulting in a blister that would ultimately turn into another long-term ulcer.

Because of the number and degree of Leigh's ulcers, he was often referred to a wound care nurse consultant while in care. Unfortunately, in the eastern area of Melbourne there was only one consultant overseeing three hospitals, so the waiting time was considerable.

Although I must point out that in 2016, during Leigh's last stay at one major hospital in Melbourne's north-east, special attention was given to his legs and back. He was given foam booties to keep his legs separated and protected, and a fully functioning air mattress – not a pinky bed mat in sight!

For me, finding the appropriate dressing was a continual learning curve and an experimental process. When Leigh was at home I would sometimes organise a visit from the Royal District Nursing Service (RDNS), as well as a private wound care nurse consultant who would advise me as to which dressing to use on which ulcer. Dressings were chosen according to the stage and size of each ulcer, but most importantly they had to adhere to his body and stay in place, given his high body temperature, particularly during the warmer weather.

During some of Leigh's hospital admissions, plastic surgeons were also asked to assess the ulcers. An MRI scan was recommended to determine the depth of one particular ulcer on his back. Sample swabs were also taken to check for infection. Many of these extra tests and scans could have been avoided had Leigh's wound care been continually addressed. Apart from the unnecessary time and expense, Leigh also had to deal with the added discomfort while already coping with other health issues.

After many years of treating Leigh's ulcers, I was desperate and prepared to trial any new therapy that seemed promising. In the early '90s, on the advice of a plastic surgeon, our first enquiry was into vibrational therapy. This treatment is very time consuming and expensive. Unfortunately, despite a prolonged period of treatment I did not see any significant improvement. However, vibrational therapy has advanced and today may have benefits for Stage 1 ulcers. Leigh's back ulcer was at Stage 3, which proved very difficult to heal using this method.

Pressure sores are described in four stages:

Stage 1 sores are not open wounds. The skin may be painful, but it has no breaks or tears. The skin appears reddened and does not blanch (lose colour briefly when you press your finger on it and then remove your finger). In a dark-skinned person, the area may appear to be a different colour than the surrounding skin, but it may not look red. Skin temperature is often warmer. And the Stage 1 sore can feel either firmer or softer than the area around it.

At **Stage 2**, the skin breaks open, wears away, or forms an ulcer, which is usually tender and painful. The sore expands into deeper layers of the skin. It can look like a scrape (abrasion), blister or a shallow crater in the skin. Sometimes this stage looks like a blister filled with clear fluid. At this stage, some skin may be damaged beyond repair or may die.

During **Stage 3**, the sore gets worse and extends into the tissue beneath the skin, forming a small crater. Fat may show in the sore, but not muscle, tendon, or bone.

At **Stage 4**, the pressure sore is very deep, reaching into muscle and bone and causing extensive damage. Damage to deeper tissues, tendons, and joints may occur.[6]

One characteristic of chronic wounds is that the tissue is hypoxic (has low oxygen levels). Wounds need oxygen to heal properly, so hyperbaric oxygen therapy (exposing the wound to 100% oxygen at a greater pressure than is normally experienced) can, in some cases, speed up the healing process. Although this treatment was recommended by a doctor at the SB clinic, we decided against it because it involved more travel and time spent away from home.

We also trialled negative-pressure wound therapy. A sealed dressing, attached to a small vacuum pump, is placed over the ulcer. The pump creates a negative pressure environment in the wound, which increases blood flow to the area and draws out excess fluid. The device is small enough to be carried by the person and can be used continuously or intermittently, depending on the type and location of the wound. Unfortunately, this device is also expensive and proved to be unsuccessful in Leigh's case.

As Leigh's ulcers increased in size and number, wound care costs also escalated, with some dressings costing up to $7.00 each (for an average size of 4 cm × 4 cm), and might only stay in place for a day or so because of perspiration or friction. On a couple of occasions the RDNS was kind enough to organise special funding

---

6   'Pressure Sores: Stages – Topic Overview' 2015, WebMD, <https://www.webmd. com/skin-problems-and-treatments/tc/pressure-sores-stages-topic-overview>.

for wound care costs through a charity organisation, which helped us enormously. I was most grateful to them.

There was also a strong odour associated with some of the dressings. Leigh became very self-conscious of this, especially during his school years, when fellow students would remark on it. A quick explanation to the teacher sometimes helped the situation.

Odor is usually caused by the breakdown of tissue. When a part of the body or section of skin is injured, anaerobic bacteria (microorganisms that do not require oxygen to thrive) move into the wound site. As they begin to methodically degrade tissue, these cells release chemicals like putrescine and cadaverine as byproducts. It's those agents that are responsible for the foul smells associated with injuries like pressure ulcers and exudating wounds.[7]

I also tried natural alternative therapies including manuka honey, which is recommended for its antibacterial properties. Essential oils, such as lavender, rosemary and tea tree, are also known for their antibacterial and healing properties. I even tried reiki, which made Leigh very relaxed!

I persevered with finding the best dressing for each stage of Leigh's ulcers. Through trial and error, I came across Hydrofera Blue foam dressing by Hollister (contact details are at the end of this book). This met all of the requirements and promoted faster healing than most of the other dressings. Within days, the edges of the ulcers were pink, indicating growth of new tissue. The dressing

---

7   'A Patient's Guide to Wound Odor', <https://advancedtissue.com/2016/02/a-patients-guide-to-wound-odor/>

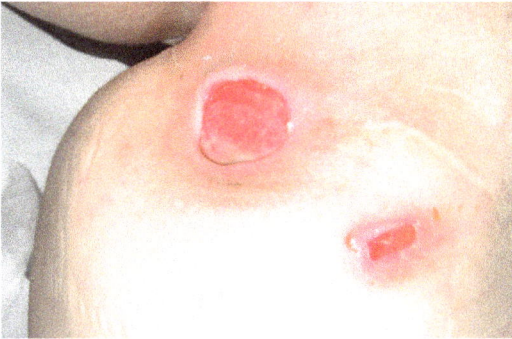

Leigh's right hip in 2014, showing the size, depth and ferocity of the ulcer before the commencement of Hydrofera Blue dressings in 2015. This ulcer continued to shrink and was about 2 cm in diameter in 2016, prior to him being readmitted to hospital.

controlled the odour and kept the fluid from the wound site contained; it was easy to use and stayed in place. We were delighted! The only drawback was that it was difficult to obtain from a local supplier, but could be sourced through the internet.

You could say I had become a reluctant sleuth on wound dressings, but my focus and drive was for Leigh to be ulcer- and pain-free – something he had not been for a long time.

While dressing his ulcers, I would always try to conceal my concern so as not to alarm or upset him, but he could read me well. He would become very frustrated and withdrawn as a result of spending hours having his ulcers dressed. It was part of the daily routine. He would never complain.

★   ★   ★

Navigating through the endless paperwork with government departments and service providers was a huge undertaking; I often wondered how others living with disabilities and their carers attained all this information. I was not always informed by medical personnel of some of the services Leigh was entitled to – more often than not, I would discover this information myself through reading articles or from talking with people in a similar position.

Up until Phillip's death in 2008, we had not sought any outside services or accepted any monetary assistance for Leigh's care. Phillip and I both had good careers and we were proud of what we had achieved on our own. We were happy to pay our own way, which is how we were both raised.

Now, the family dynamics had changed. I was worrying about Leigh's future welfare and he was worrying about me coping on my own. Leigh was on a disability support pension, which he used for things not covered by other funding, and I had a small income from my part-time employment, but this would not cover the services Leigh required. It became obvious that we needed financial help and support from outside services, so in 2009 I applied for an Individual Support Package (ISP) through the DHS.

Leigh wanted to be more independent and live away from home, sharing a house with people with similar needs, so DHS also listed him for shared supported accommodation. He also asked to be listed for respite care because he was concerned about how I would cope with his full-time care as we both grew older.

In January 2010, Leigh was granted a small amount of funding through a Linkages Package, which was monitored through a service provider.

In 2011 the service provider recommended that a case manager be appointed to organise and follow up all of the health services that Leigh required in a timely manner. Good idea! This would help us enormously in finding the appropriate services and resources he so desperately required and take some pressure off my shoulders.

A meeting was arranged for 12 September to appoint this case manager. Attending the meeting was a representative from the service provider, a therapist, an advocate for the disabled, another concerned individual who I can't remember clearly, Leigh and I. The meeting was held at a local coffee shop and amid the hustle and bustle of the trade our meeting got underway.

Everyone was eager to voice their ideas and recommendations for Leigh's wellbeing, but the central concern was accessing funds, without which none of these ideas could be put into motion. This was before the National Disability Insurance Scheme (NDIS) and Leigh was still on the waiting list for an ISP. However, despite all these good intentions and initial planning, none of these services came to fruition.

A month later the case manager had resigned and Leigh's case was handed over to another person who made infrequent contact with us. The advocate for the disabled seemed to have 'disappeared', and we never did hear from him again. The therapist was the only one who remained in contact with us. So basically we were left to our own devices again. The meeting had been set up in good faith and everyone did have Leigh's best interests at heart, but like every-thing in life people's circumstances and attitudes change, systems change and bureaucracy takes over.

★   ★   ★

It wasn't until 2015 that we received notification from DHS to say that Leigh had been short-listed for the ISP funding. I was aware that only a certain amount of funding is granted for ISP and that places only become available after a client leaves the program or passes away. So what this actually meant was that it would still be some time before Leigh would receive funding. He had been on the waiting list since 2009. Finally, in 2016, we received a trickle of ISP funds, but only after an urgent referral had been sent from a major hospital regarding Leigh's poor state of health.

I was also advised by DHS that Leigh would be fast-tracked onto the NDIS early the next year. This would have had a huge impact on his life, enabling him to acquire the services and equipment he so desperately needed in a timely manner.

None of these services were ever attained for Leigh: the waiting list was never-ending and the government money came too late.

The delay in funding for urgently needed equipment is far too long and our most vulnerable are suffering. I only hope that through schemes such as the NDIS these services become more readily accessible to those so desperately in need.

CHAPTER 9

Appointment Delays and Poor Health

There were many situations that could have had negative consequences on Leigh's health that were beyond my control, and I frequently had unsettling thoughts about them. I was particularly anxious about the delay in organising the two customised wheelchairs. It was my hope that the electric wheelchair in particular would improve Leigh's wellbeing, but deep down I knew it would take more than that. Would circumstances be different today had we been able to obtain them sooner?

I tried to keep my thoughts rational and realistic, acknowledging that Leigh's decline in health was the culmination of many factors; not least were my memories of Leigh struggling to sit upright in his chair and becoming breathless when pushing himself around.

In mid-2015 to early 2016 our search intensified to find a specialised wheelchair manufacturer that could help. The estimated cost for the electric wheelchair alone was around $25000. Partial funding for both wheelchairs was provided by SWEP and the balance was generously donated through SCOPE Victoria. Sadly, though, Leigh was never to see or use these new wheelchairs!

Leigh's kyphoscoliosis was now compromising his everyday activities. Although he could sit upright, the scoliosis tended to make him lean to one side and it was uncomfortable for him to stay in that position for any length of time. Changes to his seating systems would hopefully improve his core posture and enhance the function of his diaphragm – the main muscle of respiration – in order to expel the high levels of carbon dioxide from his body.

A rehabilitation engineer, who had been contacted through Leigh's physiotherapist, recommended a hospital clinic that specialised in treating patients with congenital disabilities such as SB, hydrocephalus, Down syndrome, etc. This clinic was considered to have the best available facilities and staff to handle Leigh's challenging requirements.

An appointment was scheduled for June 2016. Leigh was to be reviewed by the clinic's medical and allied health team before attending the wheelchair and seating clinic. However, following my phone conversations with the clinic's coordinator and the physiotherapist to discuss Leigh's overall health issues and requirements, this appointment was suddenly cancelled. I found out not from the clinic but through another physiotherapist outside the hospital who was also involved with this appointment. I did not receive any explanation for the cancellation nor was I offered another appointment. I was confused and annoyed by the clinic's actions. When I phoned to ask for an explanation and when another appointment could be rescheduled, I was told:

> ... We have already gone out of our way to schedule an early appointment for Leigh and had to reshuffle patient appointments around to fit him in. However, we find Leigh would not be

suitable to attend the clinic, as he is considered a difficult case. And as the seating and wheelchairs are very expensive, we therefore feel the resources would best benefit another patient.

I was shocked and horrified at such a callous statement coming from a healthcare professional. I was lost for words and the conversation ended abruptly. All our hopes and plans for Leigh's new wheelchairs were now seriously compromised. Her message was clear; funding had played a big part in the decision-making and appointments were limited, but her delivery was blunt, extremely unprofessional and hurtful. I felt that Leigh had been victimised by the health system.

I was now at a loss as to where we could turn. Leigh had already been to a number of wheelchair clinics and manufacturers over the years, but now he needed something unique and state-of-the-art. Fortunately, Ms Christine Blackburn, a consulting physiotherapist and friend whom we'd known since the SB clinic days, generously helped arrange an appointment with Access Health and Community, a not-for-profit organisation in Melbourne's inner east. They were obliging and eager to accommodate Leigh, even though we lived outside their catchment area. An appointment was quickly set up with a team of professional people – time was precious.

The first appointment Leigh and I attended was an initial assessment and planning session for all the team; the second appointment, at our home, was for a preliminary trial run with the specialised seating system. The third appointment, for fitting and adjustments, would follow once funding had been released.

Precious time had slipped by and it was now late August 2016. Leigh was continuing to struggle in his wheelchairs and became

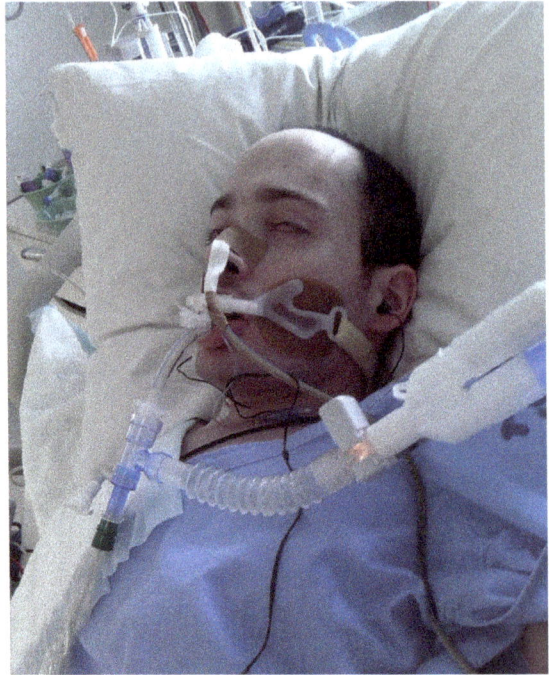

ICU in late August 2016
after intubation. Sedated
and listening to music.

unwell; he was vomiting, lethargic and had shortness of breath. He was admitted into hospital with high levels of CO_2 and a severe infection.

While in hospital his breathing became laboured and difficult, even with the help of the VPAP machine and oxygen. He was placed on a ventilator to help him expel the CO_2.

Leigh was anaesthetised for intubation (insertion of a flexible plastic tube into the trachea, or windpipe) and kept lightly sedated for pain relief. He was going through hell and all I could do was look on helplessly. I would have traded places with him in a heartbeat, but all I could do was hold his hand and try to comfort him.

While on the ventilator, Leigh had multiple seizures over an extended period of time. Doctors became concerned that his brain function may be compromised. A neurosurgeon from another hospital brought in a mobile CT scanner in order to read Leigh's brain function and check his shunts.

After an anxious wait, Jason and I were relieved to hear that everything was fine. I then asked the doctors whether Leigh was still being given his epilepsy medication (Epilim). They informed me that because this medication was in tablet form they were unable to administer it while Leigh was on the ventilator. I asked if a liquid form could be administered intravenously. After some hesitation they replied that their pharmacy did not carry it in liquid form!

With my persistence, the pharmacy ordered in the liquid Epilim and, once administered, Leigh's seizures stopped.

After a week in ICU on the ventilator, Leigh's CO_2 levels had improved and the seizures were under control. He was taken off the ventilator and monitored to see how his lungs would cope on

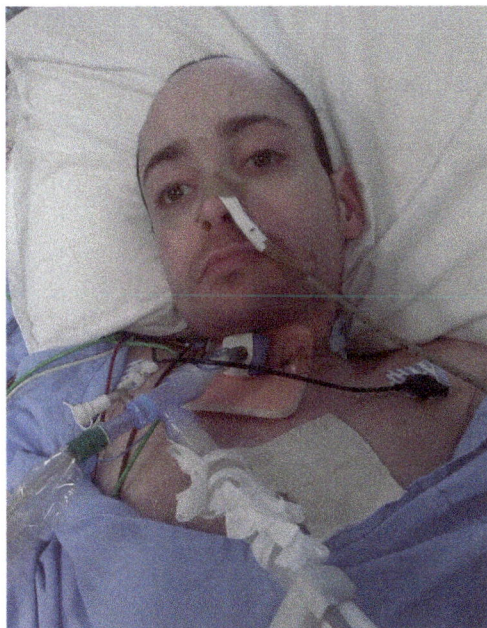

Leigh, still lightly sedated in ICU after removal of the intubation tube, now with a tracheostomy in place.

their own. However, he still struggled to maintain a constant and acceptable CO_2 level. The doctors recommended he have a tracheotomy (an incision into the neck that creates a direct airway to the windpipe) and continue with the oxygen treatment.

Leigh would not be able to speak while the tracheostomy tube was in place, so he used a signing board that had common phrases and numbers at which to point. He was going through hell, but could still manage a smile or thumbs up when I visited him each day.

After another week, with the tracheostomy tube still in place, doctors advised that Leigh would be transferred to another hospital with a specialised ward unit that provided a range of services to patients with chronic respiratory failure. Here, he would be weaned off the tracheostomy tube and oxygen.

Upon arrival, Leigh was fitted with a speaking valve, which was placed over the tracheostomy tube, enabling him to speak for the first time in over two weeks. He was delighted, giving a big and husky, 'Hooray, I can speak again!' Everyone laughed.

The tracheostomy tube was taken out after a few days and the small incision in his neck healed quickly. His CO_2 levels were regularly monitored and he spent less time on the oxygen, now only using a nasal tube.

Leigh slowly recovered and received excellent care at this unit. His pressure wound care needs were also addressed without me having to complain or intervene at any stage.

He was now ready to come home and looking forward to seeing his friends and our pets: Chloe, a Bichon Frise, and Billy, a black and white cat that we had adopted from an animal rescue shelter. He was a playmate for Chloe and would stop her fretting while Leigh and I were at work. When Chloe was a tiny puppy, I would

Chloe

Billy

lift her onto Leigh's bed and she would lick his face to wake him up. As Leigh occasionally dropped things, I also had the intention of having her trained to be his assistance dog so that she could fetch and pick things up for him and possibly learn to detect the onset of epileptic seizures. Leigh liked this idea because it would add to his independence.

I still have Chloe and Billy and whenever I am feeling sad or depressed they can sense this and will come and comfort me. Their playful antics always make me smile and laugh, just as they did for Leigh.

CHAPTER 10

Living a Nightmare

L eigh was discharged on 22 September 2016, having been away from home for a month. However, things never go to plan and it was on the way home, while I was assisting him with a manual transfer from his wheelchair into my car, that we heard a loud *pop!* My heart sank – it was the sound of either his hip dislocating or another leg fracture.

The bones in the lower part of Leigh's body were fragile at the best of times and, after being immobilised for four weeks, something as simple as a transfer could lead to a fracture. Owing to the lack of sensation, Leigh could not tell me if there was any pain, which would indicate a fracture, but deep down I feared the worst.

However, we went home and watched and waited for any signs of swelling or heat that would indicate a fracture. That night one of Leigh's legs did swell and felt hot to the touch; it was clear there was a problem that needed to be addressed, so reluctantly we went to the local hospital.

He was admitted into the Emergency Department, where the doctors were more concerned with his breathing and fast heart rate than with his leg fracture.

X-rays were taken and a fractured femur was confirmed. Usually this type of fracture would require surgery to have either a pin or plate fixed to the bone, but with Leigh's recent respiratory problems anaesthesia was not an option. Instead, doctors recommended manual traction, which meant nurses firmly holding his leg whenever he was moved in and out of bed. Leigh was now confined to bed again! He was also placed back on oxygen. I can still remember the look of complete desperation on his face when I left him that day.

The next day he was readmitted into ICU. Here, an ICU doctor discussed his concerns about Leigh's ongoing respiratory problems. This proved to be a critical discussion. He stated that there would be no ventilation intervention offered to Leigh this time at this hospital; it would be too difficult for Leigh to handle the procedure a second time, given the fact that the tracheostomy tube had been removed only recently.

I was not sure whether Leigh comprehended what the doctor was trying to explain, so I repeated everything back to him and asked the doctor to simplify his answers so that we could all grasp what he was saying.

My understanding of that discussion was that Leigh would not be ventilated and the topic of CPR was only touched on lightly.

Remembering his recent experiences, Leigh stated that he did not want to be ventilated again or have a tube inserted down his throat; he did not agree to CPR *not* being offered. There were five of us present during this discussion: Leigh, Jason, Shanta, the ICU doctor and I. I vividly remember Leigh saying that he 'did not want to die' and becoming distressed at the prospect of having another tube inserted down his throat. We all reassured him it would not come to that because he was improving and things would get better!

We were all left a little stunned by the doctor's comments. We kept thinking that Leigh would recover from his leg fracture and return home. I visited him every day and he continued to improve to the point that doctors transferred him to a general ward.

Leigh's level of care changed considerably from one-on-one specialised nursing care to having to wait an hour or more to be washed in his bed, dressed or helped onto his wheelchair. The nursing staff were overwhelmed by the number of older patients, some with cognitive problems, who required a great deal of their time and attention.

Apart from his medical needs, Leigh sometimes needed help with the simplest of things, such as when items were out of reach. Just managing meal trays or reaching for a drink could sometimes be very difficult for him, but he would never ask for assistance, instead patiently waiting for someone to come along. When I asked him why, he would tell me, 'They [the nurses] were too busy! I didn't want to worry them, and when I pressed the call button they sometimes forgot to come back to me.'

It was obvious that the staff were over-extended. The ratio of nurses to patients concerned me greatly.

A few days later, Leigh was still on and off the oxygen during the day and his leg fracture was healing. The swelling and heat in his leg had subsided and the manual traction was still being applied during transfers.

However, the pressure ulcer on his back had increased in size. I constantly requested that the wound consultant be notified in order to have it assessed, but I was again told how difficult it was to get hold of her because she was overseeing patients in three major hospitals. I found this to be unacceptable on the hospital's part.

Some time later, to my relief, I was advised that she had assessed Leigh, redressed his ulcers and would follow up when she was able. Of course, the dressings did not stay fixed in place for long and I wondered how long it would be before her next visit.

On one particular visit I was horrified when I saw the size of the ulcer on his back, so the following day I brought in my own Hydrofera Blue wound dressings to redress the ulcer. I was advised that Leigh was still waiting to be reviewed by the wound consultant.

Doctors assessed Leigh daily. One commented that he had been referred to a rehabilitation centre for recovery, but, as

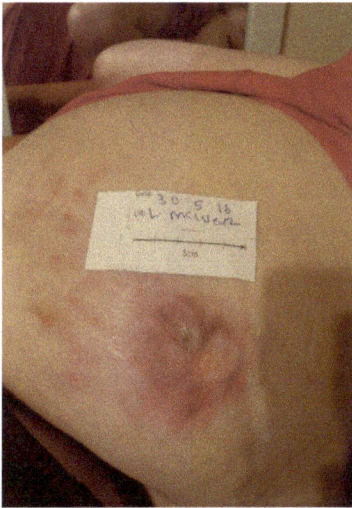

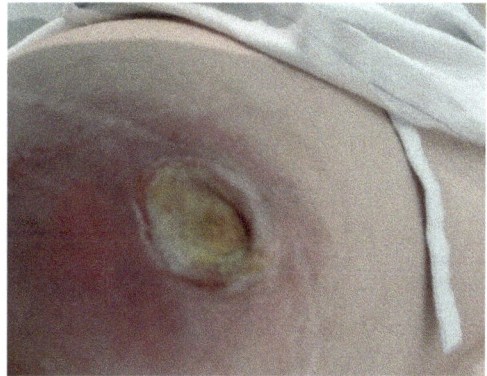

A comparison of Leigh's back ulcer: (LEFT) in May 2016 and (RIGHT) 13 October 2016. His back had been in good condition prior to his admission in late September.

always, he was on a waiting list. From the conversation with this doctor, it was my understanding that Leigh would be discharged within days. His leg fracture had healed and he was tolerating the oxygen regime, which was to be continued at home until he was feeling better.

I prepared for Leigh's return home: I organised for a wound consultant to visit and rearranged my work roster. We already had

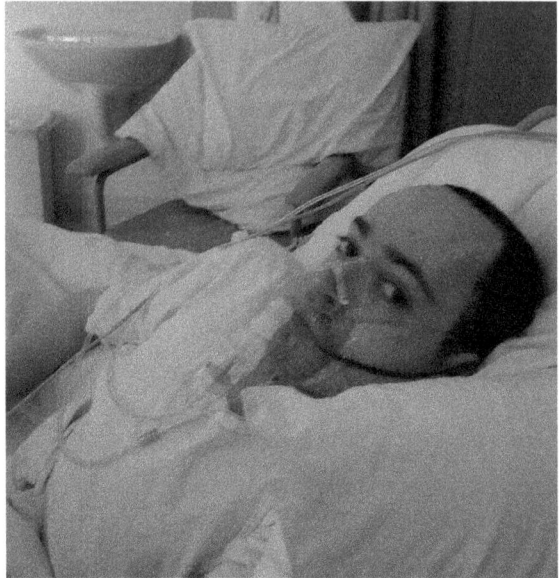

Leigh on 13 October 2016, the day before his sudden passing. It had been two weeks since this admission. I could see the look of desperation in his eyes: he just wanted to come home.

an oxygen concentrator from a previous treatment, so everything was ready.

On the morning of Friday, 14 October 2016, I visited Leigh and stayed during lunch to help with his tray, which was sometimes out of reach. We watched TV together and talked about his return home and catching up with friends.

I reluctantly left Leigh at about 2.00 pm and gave him a kiss goodbye as always. I told him I would see him again tomorrow, and that I loved him. He seemed a little agitated at me leaving this time. 'Do you have to go, Mum?' he asked. This was out of character for him – usually he did not mind me leaving – so I stayed a moment longer, fixing his bedding and adjusting the oxygen mask. I reassured him that I would see him again tomorrow and to try to get some rest. Little did I know as I looked back from the corridor that it would be the last time I would see my darling son alive …

⋆   ⋆   ⋆

It was about 9.00 pm when I received a phone call from a female doctor from the hospital. She said that a nurse had found Leigh unresponsive and that he had passed away – and then offered her condolences.

I thought someone was playing a sick joke and almost hung up – it took me a moment to comprehend who she was and what she was saying. She repeated herself and told me to come into the hospital when I was able.

I somehow managed to phone Jason and told him that the hospital had contacted me with devastating news and that we should go in straight away. Jason, Shanta and I drove to the hospital in a state of shock and were taken to a private room to see Leigh. I was living a nightmare and hoping to suddenly wake up, but it was real and I struggled to comprehend what was happening. I had just visited Leigh earlier in the day and he was fine! What had happened in the meantime?

As the nurse opened the door to the room, it was as though I were watching in slow motion. Leigh was lying in bed with his hands clasped together over his abdomen, as if he were asleep, and if I were to make a loud noise he would wake up and say, 'Hi, Mum, what are you doing?'

I placed my hands on his chest over his heart; his body was warm to touch. I waited for some sort of reaction from him, telling him to wake up and that I was here to take him home! Jason gasped a little at my comment and tried to comfort me; it was an automatic response – that of a mother – as I tried to take in what was happening.

⋆   ⋆   ⋆

The doctor who had called me at home explained the events leading up to Leigh's passing. She was a junior doctor, and I could tell from her body language and quietly spoken manner that she was inexperienced at delivering such traumatic news to a family. I was aware that locum and junior doctors are sometimes on duty during late shifts.

I listened intently, trying not to wonder whether she was experienced enough to handle an emergency like this or what course of action she had taken during the ordeal.

She proceeded to tell us that Leigh's emergency buzzer had been pressed by a nurse at 1815 hours for respiratory distress and desaturation. A medical emergency team (MET) then put him back on the VPAP machine and his oxygen intake was increased to 5 litres. According to the nurse's notes, Leigh settled; he requested a drink at 2030 hours and was given 100 millilitres of apple juice. He was to be monitored every 15 minutes. The nurse checked him at 2045 hours. Leigh was found unresponsive and there was a small amount of vomit on his gown. The nurse activated a code blue for the MET. No CPR was commenced because, according to the current Consensus Resuscitation Plan in his file, Leigh was registered as 'Not for Resuscitation'.

My body went numb and I held my breath while I listened to her describe the last moments of my son's life. As I regained focus and rational thought, my first question was, 'Why wasn't I notified at home of his initial respiratory distress?' I received no response from the doctor. Did the hospital staff think it was normal for Leigh to be so unwell, or that he had no family member who would be concerned for his welfare?

My second question was, 'Why wasn't CPR given?' The doctor explained that Leigh was registered as 'Not for Resuscitation' on the Consensus Resuscitation Plan. I was completely lost for words by the lack of detail and her handling of the situation. We needed answers that made sense.

We asked to speak with another doctor who had also been involved with Leigh's care when he was in respiratory distress. It happened to be Leigh's doctor from ICU. He came into the room and repeated a similar account of the event.

I remember thinking back to the talk we had had with him: 'no ventilation would be offered to Leigh again at this hospital'. Did this mean no CPR as well? What was their definition of 'ventilation' and 'CPR'? Was this explained to us at the time? I couldn't remember! And why did Leigh vomit? Was he unwell? Was it a seizure or maybe a heart attack? Again, we did not receive any clear answers and the doctor offered his condolences! He was then paged to return to ICU and we were again left sitting in a state of shock, denial and frustration.

My mind raced, desperately trying to interpret and understand what had happened to Leigh since lunchtime.

The first doctor briefly mentioned that Leigh had vomited while wearing his VPAP mask. Was he unable to remove the mask after vomiting? The VPAP machine would continue to push air into his lungs at set intervals and, if there was an obstruction to his airway, it would have been extremely difficult for him to clear it away. Although the control switch was next to Leigh's bed, it may not have been within reach – he may have needed help to remove the mask and to lie on his side to clear his airway! I sensed the medical staff were also shocked at Leigh's sudden passing, but this did little to ease our pain.

At this point, the doctors could not give us a clear 'cause of death' and later in the conversation suggested it was probably 'aspirational pneumonia'. I was numb with rage and could feel my heart racing, about to explode out of my chest. 'He did not have pneumonia! He was well when I left him and he did not have any of the symptoms of pneumonia, which I am familiar with from past experiences!'

On the death certificate, however, cause of death was shown as 'aspirational pneumonia (minutes)', which I now understand occurs when food, saliva or vomit is breathed into the lungs or airways instead of being swallowed. This condition was not fully explained to us on the night of Leigh's passing. I struggled to accept the cause of Leigh's death and can only link it to the apple juice he had been given while using his VPAP machine and him not being able to sit upright to cough. I have visualised this scenario many times, trying to get my head around what actually occurred that night, and it still haunts me.

I was dissatisfied because we had received insufficient information and only limited responses to my questions, so I requested an autopsy. The junior doctor left the room to call the coroner. She came back and advised us that no autopsy would be performed because the coroner was 'happy' for the death certificate to be issued due to Leigh's long medical history. Happy? What a poor choice of words coming from a doctor to describe this catastrophic event!

We spent some time with Leigh before leaving the hospital in a state of shock, anger and bewilderment at what had just occurred, and at the lack of understanding or explanation on the part of medical personnel about the events leading up to his demise. I had lost my darling son and Jason had lost his brother just eight years after Phillip's death. Our lives were shattered again!

A few days later, out of shear frustration at the absence of any clear explanation, I made a Freedom of Information request for Leigh's complete medical records from the time of his admission up to the night of his death.

Several weeks later, a disc containing more than 360 pages of handwritten nurses' and doctors' notes and accompanying paperwork arrived through the mail. I spent many hours reading the documents, trying to make some sense of what had happened to Leigh after my visit with him that day. My real fear is that I may never know or understand the true cause of his death; reading the Admissions–Discharge Summary sheet still leaves me speechless:

> Regretfully, Leigh passed away on the ward from respiratory failure after aspirating into the lungs following a large vomit. The medical decision was made not to resuscitate given Leigh's comorbidities and declining health.

Also noted on the discharge summary sheet was the fact that Leigh's GP was not notified of his passing. I thought it would be normal hospital procedure to notify the patient's doctor of a death, but particularly such a tragic and unexpected one.

* * *

A Consensus Resuscitation Plan specifies what end-of-life treatment a patient should and should not receive. I only became aware that Leigh was registered as 'Not for Resuscitation' when I read this paperwork.

CPF COPY – DO NOT MARK

CONSENSUS RESUSCITATION PLAN

CONSENSUS RESUSCITATION PLAN

UR Number: M456611
Surname: MCIVER, LEIGH   M
Given Name:
Date of Birth:

Complete either section A or B or C AND complete section D

A. Patient is for LIFE PROLONGING TREATMENT

☑ Full resuscitation with Standard MET Criteria (see below)

☐ Full resuscitation with Modified MET Criteria (complete table below)

B. Limited Resuscitation

☐ Not for CPR

☐ Not for Defibrillation

☐ Not for Intubation

☐ Not for ICU admission

☐ For Modified MET criteria

	Standard MET CRITERIA	MODIFIED MET CRITERIA
Airway	Difficulty breathing	
Breathing	RR < 8 or > 30	
	SpO$_2$ < 90% despite O$_2$ 6L/min via Hudson mask	
Circulation	HR < 50 or > 130	
	BP < 90	
	New or unrelenting chest pain	
Disability	Acute change in conscious level	
	Seizure	
Other	Worry about the patient condition	Cannot be modified

C. Patient is for PALLIATIVE treatment aimed at SYMPTOM MANAGEMENT

☐ Palliative Care Plan written and medication prescribed

D. REASON FOR DECISION

☐ Medical decision based on what is medically indicated for this patient.

Reason for decision: _____

Has patient been informed of decision? ☐Yes ☐No ☐Previously informed ☐N/A

Has family been informed of decision? ☐Yes ☐No ☐Previously informed ☐N/A

☐ Decision of competent patient

☐ Decision of person responsible (see over)

Name of Person Responsible/Legal Agent: _____ Relationship: _____

Doctor's Signature: ▮▮▮ Doctor's Name: ▮▮▮

Designation of Doctor completing this record ▮▮▮ Date 27/9/16

Authorising Consultant's Name _____

This resuscitation plan applies across all ▮▮▮ sites and is only active for this hospital admission. This plan should be reviewed regularly according to changes in clinical situation or at the request of the patient or person responsible.

The first Consensus Resuscitation Plan, dated 27 September 2016.

CPF COPY – DO NOT MARK

CONSENSUS RESUSCITATION PLAN

UF M456611
Su MCIVER, LEIGH   M
Gi
Da   / F

CONSENSUS RESUSCITATION PLAN

Complete either section A or B or C AND complete section D

A. Patient is for LIFE PROLONGING TREATMENT

☐ Full resuscitation with Standard MET Criteria (see below)

☐ Full resuscitation with Modified MET Criteria (complete table below)

B. Limited Resuscitation

☑ Not for CPR

☑ Not for Defibrillation

☑ Not for Intubation

☐ Not for ICU admission

☑ For Modified MET criteria

	Standard MET CRITERIA	MODIFIED MET CRITERIA
Airway	Difficulty breathing	
Breathing	RR < 8 or > 30	
	SpO$_2$ < 90% despite O$_2$ 6L/min via Hudson mask	
Circulation	HR < 50 or > ~~130~~	Not for tachycardia
	BP < 90	
	New or unrelenting chest pain	
Disability	Acute change in conscious level	
	Seizure	
Other	Worry about the patient condition	Cannot be modified

C. Patient is for PALLIATIVE treatment aimed at SYMPTOM MANAGEMENT

☐ Palliative Care Plan written and medication prescribed

D. REASON FOR DECISION

☑ Medical decision based on what is medically indicated for this patient.

Reason for decision: Severe permanent comorbidities

Has patient been informed of decision? ☑ Yes ☐ No ☐ Previously informed ☐ N/A

Has family been informed of decision? ☑ Yes ☐ No ☐ Previously informed ☐ N/A

☐ Decision of competent patient

☐ Decision of person responsible (see over)

Name of Person Responsible Legal Agent: _____ Relationship: _____

Doctor's Signature: _____ Doctor's Name: _____

Designation of Doctor completing this record   Intensive Care   Date 2/10/14

Authorising Consultant's Name _____

This resuscitation plan applies across all ▮▮▮▮ sites and is only active for this hospital admission. This plan should be reviewed regularly according to changes in clinical situation or at the request of the patient or person responsible.

The second Consensus Resuscitation Plan, dated 2 October 2016.

Among Leigh's medical records I found *two* Consensus Resuscitation Plans: the first dated 27 September 2016 shown as 'Full Resuscitation'; and a second dated 2 October 2016 (five days later) shown as 'Not for Resuscitation', which had been filled out after our initial meeting with the doctor in ICU. It indicated no CPR, defibrillation or intubation, but for modified MET criteria.

Other notes in Leigh's file related to the family discussion with the doctor in ICU on 2 October 2016, stating: 'patient's wishes are not for reintubation and mother present, understands and respects patient's wishes'. This was the discussion that led to the second plan ('Not for Resuscitation') being put in place. Two doctors are mentioned, but only one doctor was ever present at the discussion in ICU with Leigh, Jason, Shanta and me. There was no nurse or social worker in attendance even though the meeting took place at 11.00 am, which is within normal working hours.

It was true Leigh did not wish to be reintubated. He also stated in front of four people that he 'did not want to die'! This statement indicated that he wanted every opportunity to survive, and that medical personnel should do everything possible to make this happen. It was never Leigh's or my wish that CPR not be given in the event of a medical emergency! The difference between ventilation and CPR was not clearly explained. In the end, I am sure we all came away with a different interpretation of this meeting. The conversation was never again discussed or clarified with the family.

These two forms determined the life and death of my son. We had not previously sighted, reviewed or had any prior knowledge of them. After reading them again, they reveal that Leigh's wishes for ventilation and sustaining his life, discussed at our meeting with the doctor in ICU, had been misinterpreted.

Our family has been shattered by this experience and left wondering how many other people are also unfamiliar with the Consensus Resuscitation Plan, its contents and implications. Through Leigh's biography I wish to raise awareness that this plan exists. During my research I discovered this plan is part of the medical "Goals of Care (GOC)" assessment tool, recently being trialled in two major hospitals.

CHAPTER 11

Lost Dreams

Leigh's funeral was held on Friday, 21 October 2016 at 9.00 am. He was buried with his father, Phillip, at the Lilydale Memorial Park in eastern Melbourne.

If I had to categorise my religious beliefs I am not sure I could say with any conviction that I have a deep affinity with any particular religion. Being raised in a non-religious environment gave me the opportunity to explore my own beliefs and values later in life. I have always been empathetic and shown compassion toward both people and animals. As a youngster, I would often bring home lost or injured animals and be completely preoccupied with their welfare; and if I sighted an elderly or disabled person struggling with a simple task it would sometimes bring me to tears. These feelings were sometimes challenging and difficult to understand, but I learned to accept them and to follow my instincts.

This consideration for all living things has stayed with me and I have instilled into my own children. If I had to label my beliefs, it might be as spiritual, rather than religious. And so it was for Leigh. Accordingly, the focus for Leigh's service was structured around these ideals, as he would have wanted.

A well-known quote from the Dalai Lama sums up our life values:

This is my simple religion.
There is no need for temples;
no need for complicated philosophy.
Our own brain, our own heart is our temple;
the philosophy is kindness.

We had a celebrant read the eulogy, which I wrote myself. Family, friends and colleagues contributed moving tributes and poems, which are included at the end of this book.

Leigh's white coffin was a blank page for our final messages of eternal love for him. Guests were invited to write or draw pictures on the casket. Impulsively, I drew the outline of my hand on the coffin near his heart, symbolising my eternal care and love for him. I am not sure what others wrote, but I know it gave his family, friends and colleagues an opportunity to express their thoughts and feelings, and to say goodbye in their own way. I regret not taking photos of the day, but I was obviously not thinking very clearly at the time.

The music chosen for Leigh's service were 'happy' songs that made him smile: 'Happy' by Pharrell Williams; 'Moves like Jagger' by Maroon 5; and the WWE theme song, 'The Time Is Now' by John Cena (his WWE wrestling hero). Leigh and I would both 'dance' to these songs while sitting in the car; we would wave our arms and hands around, making funny gestures, and bop our shoulders up and down. I'm sure Leigh thought his mother had sometimes lost the plot! But our funny antics would always make him smile and that was always good to see.

At the graveside, we held thirty-three blue balloons – his favourite colour – one for every year of his precious life. As the celebrant finished his message, the coffin was lowered and together we all released our balloons into the air. As I watched them drift away, I thought for a moment, 'Where is Leigh? Has he released his balloon? Has he got a good view of the balloons floating away?' And for a second I looked around the group to check if he was okay, but then reality again hit me like a truck ...

A number of Nadrasca's managers and employees attended the funeral service. Afterwards, they posthumously awarded Leigh his Ten Year Service Award Certificate, which I very proudly accepted on his behalf. It sits in a frame next to his bed.

★ ★ ★.

Leigh had dreamed of living in supported accommodation with friends. He was an optimist who lived for the future, which gave him a purpose in life. We often discussed ways in which he could become more independent and manage his own daily care needs. Many household appliances were difficult for him to reach, and he had difficulty lifting and carrying things because of his scoliosis, but he always made an effort and would get very frustrated with himself when things didn't go the way he planned.

He enjoyed cooking – his favourite meals were pasta, noodles and toasted cheese sandwiches. In the kitchen we had a height-adjustable table where he could comfortably use a portable hot plate, and on the bench we had a microwave oven and small conventional oven within easy reach that he used to whip up some tasty meals. These seemingly small accomplishments were a major undertaking for Leigh; the satisfaction and pleasure it gave him was enormous.

Leigh and I tried to pack as much as we could into our weekends. We would often go to the local shopping centre for lunch and then browse through all the computer game stores in search of that perfect wrestling game. He was an avid supporter of all things WWE, whether playing it on his computer or watching it on television. He also collected the wrestling figurines, which he continually told me, 'Keep them in their original packaging so they'll hold their value!' He attended a couple of live WWE events in Melbourne in 2016, accompanied by a support worker, and on another occasion in 2012 with Simon, his friend from Nadrasca.

Leigh loved going to the cinema, with his friends or just on his own, to see the latest action or comedy movies.

He also enjoyed gardening so we built a raised garden bed for him to try his hand at growing herbs and vegetables. He was very proud of his garden, and we would pick and cook veggies together.

Leigh had so much potential; he was not defined by either his physical condition or health issues. He was always eager to help anyone in need and often became frustrated when his desire to render assistance was thwarted by his physical limitations. He spoke proudly about how he helped a work colleague who was having a seizure while sitting at a table. He was able to move obstacles out of the way, check his airway and then call for staff members to assist. This was his beautiful nature and, sadly, the only person he ever became angry and frustrated with was himself.

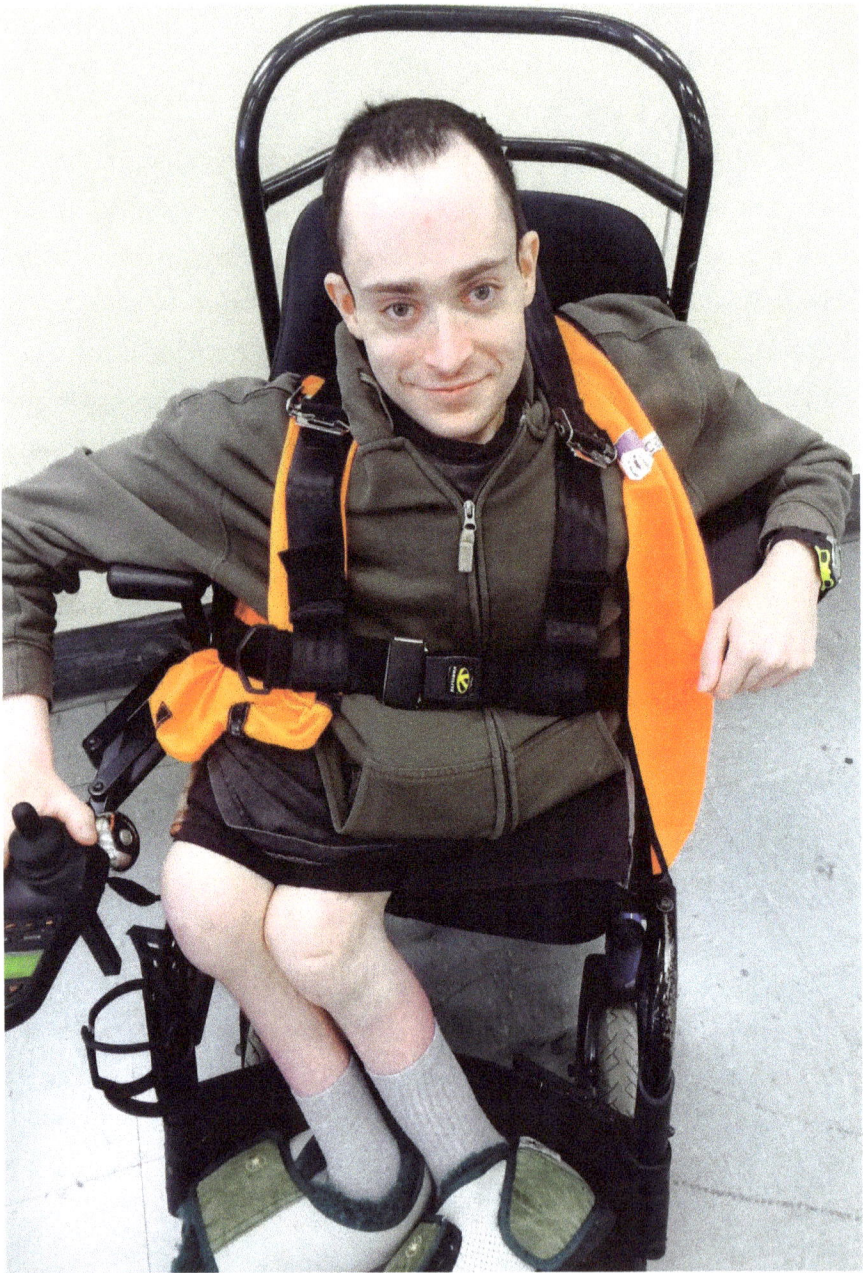

CHAPTER 12

A Look Inside Our Hospital System

I have learnt some hard lessons over the years. Foremost was to recognise that doctors and nurses are human and mistakes can happen. It is unfortunate that I did not perceive this sooner; I could have taken steps to avoid certain procedures or treatments, or at least obtained a second opinion about some of Leigh's care. It is difficult looking back and writing about these events now, thinking that maybe I should have gone with my gut instinct more often and said no, or looked more closely at diagnoses and treatments, or just intervened!

While observing Leigh's medical care and living through my late husband's heart attack, my confidence in the medical fraternity has been constantly tested. I will share a few experiences Leigh encountered while under hospital care.

Fundamentally, however, this is not about accountability, but about showing gaps or failings in routine procedures, and how easily they can go wrong, with the intention of facilitating improvement to patient care. Some of these instances are the result of human error and possibly inadequate training or experience; others are about lack of equipment and staff shortages through insufficient funding.

★   ★   ★

The pain and anguish Leigh suffered was not always caused by his condition.

As a child, he had many leg fractures resulting from weak bones. On one occasion an orthopaedic technician in a major hospital re-fractured Leigh's healed leg while removing the plaster cast. The familiar sound of breaking bone was a clear indication. The rough handling that caused this was inexcusable; the technician's training should have prepared them for working with patients with weak bones. A replacement cast was required, but the technician had the last word by commenting, 'The previous cast had not been set correctly in the first place.' One will never know!

We then had to endure additional weeks of Leigh being in a cast. I remember carrying him around on my hip from bathroom to bedroom; getting him in and out of the car; managing pressure sores from the plaster rubbing on his skin; and trying to balance a board on his wheelchair to accommodate the plaster.

In another major hospital, and as an adult, Leigh required a permanent catheter during a prolonged stay in the ICU. During my visit I noticed his urine (in the drainage bag attached to his bed) was bright red. I thought he might have been prescribed a medication that caused this. I alerted a nurse who later advised me that the ICU doctor who inserted the catheter had 'difficulty getting it in'! This ineptitude caused a great deal of trauma to Leigh's urethra and he continued to bleed for two days; subsequently he was given a course of antibiotics in case of infection. Because Leigh had no sensation in the lower part of his body he was unable to feel the procedure and hence tell the doctor that all was not well, but the doctor should have been aware of this and asked for assistance.

Mistakes will, of course, happen from time to time. At this same hospital, a nurse on the general ward had hurriedly administered Leigh's antibiotics intravenously through the line in his arm and then left the room to attend to another patient. The antibiotic fluid slowly leaked out around the insertion site onto the sheets. As soon as I noticed this, I tracked down a nurse to tell her what had happened; by this time Leigh had only received half the antibiotic dose he was prescribed, but no apology or corrective dose was given.

I started to wonder how many other mishaps had occurred when I was not with him. Leigh was never one to complain about his care; he trusted and accepted that the nurses and doctors knew what they were doing.

As a frequent onlooker I have observed hospital wards operating at full capacity, often with minimal nursing staff trying to cope with patient needs within an unrealistic timeframe. Unfortunately this can lead to rushed care, which in turn may cause additional stress to the patient.

★   ★   ★

I noticed that in many hospitals basic aids were limited; patients and nursing staff were often left frustrated. For example, self-help poles, either free-standing or attached to beds, were not available in certain hospitals for patients to use when repositioning themselves in bed. Therefore, Leigh found it difficult to pull himself up to relieve the pressure on his back or bottom and, as a consequence, was susceptible to additional pressure ulcers occurring, even while on an air mattress. Instead, he would have to lean on his arms and elbows to push himself upwards in bed, resulting in red and inflamed skin.

Mobile bed hoists with appropriate slings were also limited in the general wards. In addition, the waiting time for a mobile hoist with available staff to assist would sometimes be hours during the busy morning periods!

★   ★   ★

Toileting is one of the most basic aspects of patient care. I visited Leigh daily and would sometimes find him sitting in a wet bed. Seeing him in such a state was upsetting; while it was frustrating for me, it was humiliating for Leigh as an adult.

Showering is another basic part of a patient's overall care and wellbeing that should be offered daily to those well enough, but still in need of assistance. Clinical studies have shown that bathing patients is the best way to reduce bacteria, help prevent hospital-acquired infections and to assess patients for skin breakdown that may lead to pressure ulcers.

During Leigh's many long hospital stays as an adult, he was showered by staff only a few times that I can remember, and was generally washed while on his bed, even after he had recovered from an illness or surgery. I often asked why he had not been offered a shower and was told that it was because there were insufficient staff. On most occasions I showered and toileted him myself, even when he was in ICU, and also helped him clean his teeth and shave.

There was one occasion when Leigh was showered by a team of nurses that left me speechless. I was very thankful for their efforts, but it became a mammoth undertaking. I stepped back and watched the nurses, squashed into a small bathroom, all offering their input on how to manage the commode chair, the hoist, the sling and the drip lines. Leigh, still feeling poorly, was trying to hold his composure and keep his dignity while naked and surrounded by all these nurses; it could have been a farcical sketch from a sitcom if it weren't so heartbreaking to watch!

I had been showering Leigh at home on my own for many years yet, within the hospital system, it took a team of people to fulfil the same task, occupational health and safety notwithstanding.

Leigh was often prescribed laxatives, which I advised against due to his loss of bowel movement sensation and control. Staff soon realised their error when it came time to clean him up; I was usually there to assist them. This was all very stressful for Leigh and it continually happened with each hospital admission.

★   ★   ★

Phillip and I had put our son's life into the hands of many trained professionals, but some surgical procedures and treatments did not have a favourable outcome. In the early years, we did not complain or question the doctors' treatments or advice. Reflecting on this now, I can only relate this to my upbringing when, back in the '60s, we were taught to respect people in authority and to not question their advice. I have since come to learn that this approach did little to help either Leigh or Phillip and our quest for excellent medical care.

Over the years, Leigh's overall healthcare needs were addressed to some degree through numerous doctors' referrals and appointments across three different hospitals and several hospital clinics.

When we first entered the system, the healthcare and treatments for children with SB were monitored through the SB clinic. But this was a paediatric outpatient clinic, so when a child turned eighteen, these needs became the sole responsibility of the parent or carer. Since then a 'transitional service' for children going into adulthood has been established. This service would have been of great assistance to us.

Trying to find the right services for Leigh was a daunting task. With no professional medical training, I went with my own instincts as a mother. Mostly, I turned to our local GP who, not being specialised in specific areas relating to SB, often prescribed inappropriate medications. For example, he prescribed antacid medication for an occasional night-time cough and wheezing. I later discovered that this may have been an early symptom of hypoxaemia and should have been further investigated.

Keeping Leigh up-to-date with his medications and appointments was a constant daily and weekly routine: he took numerous medications throughout the day; and had many appointments that had to be coordinated around his school or work and around my work roster. He attended an epilepsy clinic, a clinic for the VPAP machine, respiratory clinic, psychiatric appointments, gastroenterology clinics and wheelchair fittings.

★   ★   ★

Hospital car parking, or lack thereof, is an incidental facility that most visitors would have experienced.

Every major hospital Leigh and I attended had similar problems. The shortage of disabled parking spaces was particularly problematic, yet this could easily be rectified. Parking fees were excessive and time intervals, if applicable, were inappropriate, particularly when you consider the time it takes to walk to and from an appointment, and allow for doctors to be running late, or any unforeseen delays.

However, I must acknowledge that some hospitals offer a concession rate parking permit to families in cases of long-term care or financial hardship. This is approved through the hospital's social services and not openly communicated. This was a huge saving for us and much appreciated. So if you have to visit a particular hospital it is worth checking whether they can offer any concessions.

★　★　★

I must emphasise here that I do not wish to appear ungrateful or self-centered in my views around the medical system. I am highlighting experiences which I felt could have been easily corrected or avoided through funding, expertise, or in some cases, "common sense". Over many years across three different hospitals Leigh did encounter exceptional nursing care. The treatments were administered in a professional and courteous manner with some nurses going that extra distance in organizing items or services for Leigh to help reduce his boredom.

Phillip and I were also grateful to Miss Elizabeth Lewis, Leigh's neurosurgeon, for her unrelenting determination and care during the many shunt revisions in the early years, and the numerous doctors and therapists who gave up their Saturdays to undertake the Spina Bifida Clinics.

Another, professional who was foremost in Leigh's wellbeing and who also instigated many of the orthopaedic appointments and other services during Leigh's adult life, was Ms Christine Blackburn (Consulting Physiotherapist).

I recall one experience with Leigh as a small child sheepishly revealing to me a twenty cent coin he had obtained after a consultation with Christine. I'm not sure how he came to receive his "reward", but this was indicative of how relaxed and friendly the SB clinics were organized which helped to reduce the level of stress parents were sometimes under.

Leigh was always attentive and keen to be involved in the discussions around his care, and as a child he was quick to pick up on medical and orthopaedic terminology which he later demonstrated at school by describing what a "patella" was, and then confidently pointing to his kneecap.

The dedication and support shown to Leigh, especially during his childhood years, was irreproachable. This however was not always the case during his adult years while accessing mainstream health services.

I will always be grateful to all those exceptional people associated with Leigh's care, who were part of the never-ending fight and struggle to help him obtain a good quality of life – compassion, dedication and respect are qualities that cannot be taught in any classroom.

CHAPTER 13

Affirmation

Through my investigations at the time of writing this book into the Consensus Resuscitation Plan which is part of the GOC, I now understand that every patient admitted into a public hospital is under the bed care of a doctor – the assistant medical officer (AMO) – who has both the medical and legal responsibility for that patient. The AMO (or their delegate) must clarify with other medical staff – including the patient's GP and other health practitioners who may have known that patient for many years – details of the patient's background, ongoing management and any Advance Care Directive (ACD), which would include specific instructions regarding resuscitation.

In Leigh's case, the hospital in which Leigh died never asked his GP whether an ACD had been put in place – I assume this was because of his pre-existing medical history with that particular hospital. However, neither was an ACD ever mentioned or discussed during any of Leigh's hospital admissions or consultation appointments throughout his adult years!

An **Advance Care Directive** is a legal form that allows people over the age of 18 years to write down their wishes, preferences and instructions for future healthcare, end of life, living arrangements and personal matters and/or appoint a substitute decision-maker to make these decisions on their behalf when they are unable to do so themselves.[8]

I only became aware of an ACD from an ICU nurse during Leigh's last admission, when she briefly asked if doctors had approached us about organising one. This was the first time we'd heard of such a plan. In hindsight, if this had been in place it would have clearly conveyed his wishes for ongoing management and resuscitation to the MET and all other medical personnel who had access to his records.

I also understand and appreciate that an ACD would have to be reviewed regularly to reflect any changes in a patient's circumstances and medical condition.

I was also surprised that neither the patient nor their substitute decision-maker is given an opportunity to review the Consensus Resuscitation Plan, neither are they required to sign it.

Since reading through Leigh's medical records, I felt compelled to email the hospital and outline my concerns about their routine procedures and the handling of events leading up to his death. I strongly recommended that amendments be made to the Consensus Resuscitation Plan. I also suggested that patients and family members needed to be made aware of the existence of the plan; and that the contents, options and implications be fully explained.

8   'About [Advance Care Directives]' 2014, Advance Care Directives, Government of South Australia, <https://advancecaredirectives.sa.gov.au/about>.

Some months later, a hospital liaison officer offered to set up a meeting between the hospital staff who had been directly involved in Leigh's care, me and any family member wishing to attend. The purpose of the meeting was to clarify any misleading information we had been given; discuss my concerns about the hospital Consensus Resuscitation Plan; examine the procedures for filling out the form; and assess the implementation of the plan with regard to Leigh's wishes and care.

She commented, 'It would be good to hear the human side of what happened that night.' I hesitated at first, but on reflection I realised that this was the only way to have the many nagging questions answered. I worked up the courage to accept her invitation to meet with the medical personnel at a neutral location. I would be speaking not only on Leigh's behalf, but on behalf of other unfortunate families who may experience similar circumstances in the future. I was fully aware that I would probably be out of my depth in describing medical issues and would no doubt overstep boundaries when advising senior doctors about their medical procedures and protocols. However, I was going there to discuss what had happened to my son and to express my concerns for future sons and daughters who may one day access this hospital system, so it was important that my message be heard.

The meeting was held on 22 August 2017, ten months after Leigh's passing. In attendance were two senior ICU doctors, the liaison officer, Jason and I. Both doctors listened intently while I nervously read my prepared statement and list of questions; I waited for their reaction and response. They both offered their condolences and then acknowledged their concern over some of the treatment

Leigh and our family had experienced. They also apologised for the hospital not notifying us earlier in the evening when Leigh first became unwell.

I noted their apology, but it had little impact or meaning for me – 'sorry' was just a nondescript word; a word I did not recall hearing very often from medical personnel.

Between them, the doctors explained that Leigh's oxygen levels were going down and his CO_2 levels were going up, and that he had poor reserves; he was just 'holding his own', and that in retrospect, CPR would have caused tremendous injury because the scoliosis had affected the structure of his rib cage.

They commented that Leigh was always going to pass away from respiratory problems and not from cardiac issues, adding that it is difficult to gauge the best course of action when there is no specific potential outcome for a patient. The high CO_2 levels would have made him very drowsy and, with the small amount of aspirate after drinking the apple juice, he was unable to recover because he had no reserves.

'The aspirate would have gone into his lungs,' one doctor said. Leigh's heart had stopped. No heartbeat was found, so they were unable to shock Leigh's heart back into a normal rhythm. CPR, which involves chest compressions, was not a viable option either and might have caused serious trauma, leaving Leigh in severe pain or worse.

If there had been enough reserve, Leigh could have coughed up the aspirate and cleared his lungs. He was also 'intermittently desaturated', meaning his blood oxygen level was too low and therefore his body would have been unable to deal with this trauma.

The other doctor explained that Leigh's oxygen level had been recorded at 86–88%, and that if any one of us had a similar reading our bodies would have given up!

I listened closely and hung on every word, visualising my son trying to take his last breaths alone. I sat frozen in time, reliving the moment, and slowly began to accept that even if CPR had been administered the outcome would not have changed. It was extremely difficult to hear, but necessary for me to understand.

The explanation of Leigh's low oxygen levels was not new information to me, but the degree and severity of his problems were. His failing health was never conveyed to me during any of my last visits, and the plans for his homecoming had only encouraged and strengthened my (and Leigh's) belief that he was getting better.

One doctor commented that he and the ICU team were sad that Leigh had passed away and that they had worked hard to get him better. He was also disappointed that I, as Leigh's mother, was not aware how sick he was. He discussed the Consensus Resuscitation Plan, adding that it wasn't so much about the form, but the fact that the family should have been told by the registrar exactly what was involved so that everyone was on the same page.

He was disappointed that we didn't understand that CPR was *not* a viable option for Leigh, saying 'at the end of the day we should have made you understand!', for which he apologised.

He told us that a second opinion had been arranged for Leigh on 12 October, when a medical team from another hospital that Leigh had previously attended came to assess him. They recommended a CT scan with a contrast dye, to look at the lungs, which was done the following day.

CONSENSUS RESUSCITATION PLAN

UR Number: _____

Surname: _____

Given Name: _____

Date of Birth: ___/___/___   Sex: M / F

(Affix Hospital I.D. Label if Available)

Advance Care Plan/Directive available for this patient (Check EMR or legal tab in CPF)   Yes ☐   No ☐

Substitute Decision Maker*

Name _____

Relationship to patient _____

MANAGEMENT PLAN for this patient: (Select one: tick blue, grey or pink section)

☐ **All ward treatment with FULL RESUSCITATION, if required.**
Goals of care are to cure disease and restore function.
For cardiopulmonary resuscitation (CPR)

☐ **All ward treatment with LIMITED RESUSCITATION.**
Goals of care are to cure disease and/or restore function.
NOT FOR CPR but this patient is for other active management.
Consider ICU Referral Yes ☐   No ☐
Other escalation treatments: (Refer to notes on reverse) _____
_____
_____

☐ **SYMPTOM TREATMENT**
Goals of care are comfort and quality of life.
NOT FOR CPR but is for best supportive care

MET CRITERIA Complete MET modifications, as applicable.

	Standard MET CRITERIA	MODIFIED MET CRITERIA
Airway	Difficulty breathing	
Breathing	RR < 8 or > 30	
	SpO$_2$ < 90% despite O$_2$ 6L/min via Hudson mask	
Circulation	HR < 50 or > 130	
	Systolic BP < 90	
	New or unrelenting chest pain	
Disability	Acute change in conscious level	
	Seizure	
Other	Worry about the patient's condition	Cannot be modified

Goals of care discussed with: Patient ☐   Substitute Decision Maker / Family ☐

OR Previously discussed ☐

OR Not discussed ☐   State reason: _____

Doctor: (Print name) _____

Designation: Registrar ☐   Consultant ☐   GP ☐   HMO (in consultation with Registrar/Consultant) ☐

Signature: _____   **Pager:** _____   **Date:** _____   **Time:** _____

Consultant Medical Practitioner responsible for decision: (Print name) _____

Print Media Group EH-NG0RFMR0005 05/17

CONSENSUS RESUSCITATION PLAN

The revised Consensus Resuscitation Plan now used by two major hospitals in Melbourne together with instructions for completing the form.

CONSENSUS RESUSCITATION PLAN	UR Number: _____
	Surname: _____
	Given Name: _____
	Date of Birth: ___/___/___ Sex: M / F
	(Affix Hospital I.D. Label if Available)

GUIDE TO COMPLETING CONSENSUS RESUSCITATION PLAN (CRP)

Medical Assessment:

- What is the likely diagnosis? Does this patient have a potentially reversible (treatable) illness?
- Will treatment cure this patient's illness and or restore his/her function?
- Will escalation of treatment help, if serious clinical deterioration or complication arises?
- What are the patient's preferences, wishes, and life goals? Does he/she have an advance care plan? Can he/she participate in discussions? If not, who is the substitute decision maker?
- Discuss treatment options, likely outcomes, and patient preferences for this admission.

Select one of the three options on the form that best describes the most appropriate management plan for this patient:

1. All ward treatment with full resuscitation, if required.

Goals of care are to cure disease and restore function. For the majority of (acute or elective) patients this option will be the most appropriate selection. When in doubt, (e.g. the medical assessment answers are unclear) select this option.

2. All ward treatment with limited resuscitation.

Goals of care are to cure disease and/or restore function but escalation of treatment may not benefit, or has been declined, by this patient. Document the nature of the limitation(s).
Consider the following common **escalation of treatment** options:

- Modification of MET call criteria.
- Respiratory support e.g. mechanical ventilation, non-invasive ventilation.
- Circulatory support e.g. vasopressor infusion.
- Renal support e.g. acute dialysis.
- Referral and/or transfer to ICU or CCU.
- Referral and/or transfer to other acute-care service.
- Major surgery.
- Antibiotics, nutritional support, etc.

3. Symptom Treatment.

Goals of care are comfort and quality of life with best supportive care.

NOTES:

- This form is valid for the current admission only, with the exception of patients attending regularly to ▮▮▮▮ ▮▮▮▮ Facilities for Haemodialysis or Residential Aged Care where it is valid for 12 months.
- A resuscitation alert (care order) must be completed in the patient's electronic medical record (EMR).
- If changes are required, complete a new CRP form and mark the old form "VOID" and print name and date.
- The details of CRP discussions should be clearly documented in the patient's current progress notes.

Patient transfer between ▮▮ sites or change of care type:
If a patient is transferred between ▮▮ sites, or a new episode of care is commenced during the same admission, the CRP decision is valid during transfer. Upon arrival a new CRP form should be completed within 72hours. If the patient's clinical state is unchanged, the information may be transcribed from the old form and discussion with the patient/family need not be repeated.

Substitute decision maker: Person appointed or identified by law to make decisions on behalf of a person whose decision-making capacity is impaired.

Adapted from the Royal Hobart Hospital, Monash Health, and Northern Health Goals of Care Plan

Rear page of revised Consensus Resuscitation Plan.

Information Sheet

Cardiopulmonary Resuscitation (CPR)

If you have any English language difficulties, please ask staff to book an interpreter.
From home contact the Telephone Interpreter Service on 9605 3056.
Services are provided free of charge. Ask staff if this information is available in your preferred language.

INFORMATION FOR PATIENTS, FAMILIES AND CARERS

This information sheet has been developed for patients, families and their carers to help make decisions about CPR (Cardiopulmonary Resuscitation). We hope it will be useful for you.

What is CPR?

CPR is an emergency intervention that tries to restart a person's heart and breathing if they stop. This can be a medical emergency but for many it is a natural process at end of life. CPR (commonly known as an "arrest") involves:

- Compressing the chest to pump blood around the body.
- Assisting breathing with the use of a mask or tube.
- Using a defibrillator to try and restart the heart.
- Using medication to help restart the heart.

Why do I need to think about CPR?

Most people who are admitted to hospital will get better with time and will be able to go home. Unfortunately, some people remain very unwell and they may die from their illnesses. Not uncommonly, patients in hospital become critically ill without warning, causing their breathing and/or their heart to stop. This is called "cardiopulmonary arrest".
When a person's heart and breathing stop suddenly, the doctors and nurses need to decide whether to give an emergency treatment called "cardiopulmonary resuscitation" (CPR). Sometimes CPR can be very helpful and the person will recover so that they are able to leave hospital. At other times, CPR will not work or will leave that person in a worse situation. Planning what will happen to a person who has a cardiopulmonary arrest is a normal part of good hospital care.

If I did have an arrest, will CPR help me?

How helpful CPR is depends on the cause of the arrest and on your other health problems. Everybody is different and your health care team will explain if CPR could be helpful for you.

Who decides if I get CPR?

You and your doctor(s) may decide together whether CPR should be attempted if you arrest. Some factors that might influence this decision include:

- Underlying health conditions
- Your wishes
- Current illness/injury

If you want, your close friends and family can help with this decision.
It is established policy that should a person suffer an arrest in hospital, CPR would be performed unless it has been decided otherwise.

Who makes the decision about CPR if I am too unwell to decide for myself?

If you cannot make the decision for yourself your family or significant others may be able to decide for you. They know you personally, your healthcare team will talk to them to understand your wishes and beliefs.
Some people have nominated or appointed a person/s to make medical decisions on their behalf if ever they were in a situation where they could not make decisions for themselves, for example an Enduring Power of Attorney (Medical Treatment). Your doctor will always talk through the decision with your legally appointed person/s, family or carers if this is possible.

1/1

The new Cardiopulmonary Resuscitation information sheet.

What if I don't want CPR?

If you don't want CPR, you can refuse it and the health care team must follow your wishes. Your doctor will write this in your medical record. However, you can change your mind at any time while you are still able to make your own decisions.

Some people also make an **advance care directive.** This can either be told to someone or better still, written down. If you have an advance care directive you must make sure that the health care team knows about it and puts a copy of it in your records. You should also encourage people close to you to tell the health care team about your wishes if they were asked. It is advisable to write an advance care directive in discussion with a health professional who knows you well such as your GP.

What if I want CPR to be attempted, but my doctor says it won't work?

When you discuss CPR your doctor may say that CPR would not work for you.

- No doctor will refuse your wish for CPR *if* there is a fair chance that it can be effective.
- If your healthcare team feel CPR will not work for you, you can ask them to arrange a second medical opinion if you would like one.
- In most cases, doctors and their patients, family or carers agree about CPR decisions where there has been good communication.
- You and those closest to you should be aware that there is no legal right to demand any treatment that will not work.

When a decision not to try CPR has been made?

If you have decided you do not wish CPR to be attempted, or if your doctor is sure CPR will not work, this will be documented in your medical record. This decision is about CPR **only**. Your healthcare team will continue to give you the best possible care and treatment.

Who else can I talk to about this?

If you feel that you have not had the chance to have a proper discussion with your health care team please tell them this and try again. If you are still not happy with the discussions it can be arranged for you to talk to someone else. In the first instance discuss your concerns with the manager of your ward. Here are some other people who can provide assistance:
- Those closest to you
- A social worker
- A spiritual carer (such as a chaplain)
- A cultural advisor
- EH Patient Relations
- Your GP

If you have any questions and would like to discuss this information further, please let a member of your health care team know.

For more information re Advance Care Planning (ACP):

- Department of Health ACP website and FAQ www.health.vic.gov.au/acp/
- Office of the Public Advocate Advice Service 1300 309 337 www.publicadvocate.vic.gov.au

References:
"Sharing and Involving" Information for patients and their carers to help make decisions about CPR (Cardiopulmonary Resuscitation) - GIG CYMRU NHS Wales Feb 2015
Deciding about Resuscitation Information for Patients, Family / Whānau - Canterbury Health Nov 2011

He also mentioned that the Advance Care Directive assessment would have been planned during his rehabilitation.

One of the doctors then produced two forms, stating "In the last couple of months of Leigh's passing, changes have been made to the Consensus Resuscitation Plan. These new forms are currently being used in two major hospitals". (New forms on previous pages).

He commented that he would take our discussion to their registrars in ICU and explain to them that our perception of that initial meeting in ICU was different to the doctor's.

He went on to explain that the Consensus Resuscitation Plan was a reflection of what was discussed at the meeting ... and no, the family does not see the completed form. 'Whatever happens at the meeting is what happens on the form.'

He informed us that usually a social worker is present at such family meetings. He was not sure why a social worker had not been in attendance and that if the meeting had been held in the middle of the night then one might not have been available. He was also unsure why a social worker had not been not present after Leigh's passing. 'Maybe this was due to after hours.'

Our initial meeting with the ICU doctor regarding Leigh's condition actually occurred late morning, but the meeting with doctors after Leigh's passing did occur after 9.00 pm.

The doctor then handed us a copy of the revised Consensus Resuscitation Plan and an accompanying information sheet on CPR, which would be issued to patients, families and carers covering all aspects of CPR in plain terminology.

Jason and I were surprised that our message had been taken seriously and actioned upon so quickly. I believe these two senior doctors were also keen advocates for these changes.

★   ★   ★

I commend these two doctors for their efforts. After all, we are all striving for the same outcome – better patient care.

A 'Goals of Care' Plan, which includes a resuscitation plan if applicable, has been trialled in two hospitals:

Summary

- A novel clinical framework called 'goals of care' (GOC) has been designed as a replacement for not-for-resuscitation orders. The aim is to improve decision making and documentation relating to limitations of medical treatment.

- Clinicians assign a patient's situation to one of three phases of care — curative or restorative, palliative, or terminal — according to an assessment of likely treatment outcomes ... the default position is the curative or restorative phase.

- GOC helps identify patients who wish to decline treatments that might otherwise be given, such as treatment with blood products. This includes patients for whom specific limitations apply because of their beliefs.

- GOC has been introduced at Royal Hobart Hospital, Tasmania, and at Northern Health, Melbourne. So far, audit data and staff feedback have been favourable. There have been no reported major incidents or complaints in which GOC has been causally implicated in an adverse outcome.[9]

At the time of writing, in Victoria there is an assessment procedure for all patients.

---

9   'Goals of care: a clinical framework for limitation of medical treatment', <https://www.mja.com.au/journal/2014/201/8/goals-care-clinical-framework-limitation-medical-treatment>

Identify goals of care when the patient is admitted:

- The treating team works with the patient and family to identify goals of care.
- Goals of care inform medical decision-making and limitations of medical treatment (resuscitation plan).
- Medical management aligns with the patient's values and preferences from the point of admission.

Revisit goals of care when:

- the patient is readmitted to hospital
- there are significant changes in the patient's condition or circumstances
- the patient, substitute decision-maker or family request it
- the patient, substitute decision-maker or family expresses concerns.

About goals of care:

- Active medical treatments and end-of-life care are not mutually exclusive.
- Goals of care are reflected in the clinical treatment plan, limitations of medical treatment (resuscitation plan) and advance care planning.[10]

---

10 'Goals of care', Department of Health and Human Services, <https://www2.health. vic.gov.au/hospitals-and-health-services/patient-care/end-of-life-care/palliative-care/essential-elements/goals>

CHAPTER 14

Reflections

My heart still aches at not being with Leigh during his final moments. Accepting the hospital's apology has been difficult. However, these doctors did acknowledge and recognise the hospital's failure in not notifying us when Leigh became unwell, and showed genuine remorse. It was also apparent during this meeting that Leigh's sudden passing was unexpected and a shock to the attending medical staff.

Jason and I welcome the changes made to the hospital's end-of-life documentation, and we hope hospitals continue to listen and act upon concerns raised by patients and their families in an effort to enhance patient care.

Over the years, Leigh and I battled the effects of his disability. SB is not one condition; it is a multitude of problems that affect the mind, the body and the spirit. No two cases are the same. It is a relentless and unforgiving condition.

Leigh and I cried and laughed together when his illnesses and the many obstacles became overwhelming. One aspect of our special bond was the quirky sense of humour that we developed to alleviate the frustration we both felt – people might be surprised at what amused us! I would have traded places with Leigh in a heartbeat to free him from the wheelchair, the medical procedures and surgeries, the medication, the breathing equipment and the suffering.

We were always searching for new therapies and advances in medical procedures and mobility technology that would hopefully improve his health and wellbeing. Leigh often talked and day-dreamed about finding just the right equipment that would help him fulfil his hopes and dreams. Following in his father's footsteps, he sketched intriguing wheelchair designs with hoists and pulley devices that would enable him to stand, or lift and move heavy objects. He took great delight in giving detailed explanations of his creations and how he would use them at work.

The effects of the SB slowly overtook his body, never releasing its insidious grip; so he could explore and fulfil all his hopes and dreams. A quiet, softly spoken, self-effacing man, who struggled to live life to the full.

Leigh never had the opportunity to experience a long-term relationship with a life partner. For many people living with a disability, life can be lonely and isolating, restricted not only by physical and psychological barriers, but by social and economic circumstance.

Similarly, full-time caregivers can experience social isolation, anxiety and depression. I applaud all caregivers and parents for their endless courage and selfless efforts. Many carry on alone, often in silence, as they try to manage the constant daily needs of a loved one. Some may be so driven by an overwhelming moral responsibility, by pride, or by the love and the instinct to protect that they may be unwilling or unable to seek outside assistance.

I struggled with many of these feelings and never sought help until Leigh and I were much older. In the last few years of his life I finally accepted that I could not do it all on my own, but quickly discovered that respite care and in-home services were far more difficult to organise than I had anticipated. I approached a number of agencies and government departments with requests for help, and again and again encountered endless waiting lists and funding shortfalls; the many obstacles that arose when organising multiple services for Leigh's complex medical needs were overwhelming.

So I urge all caregivers to seek help if you are struggling and to continue to push for it, even when you are turned away by government departments or allied services. More services, both ongoing and respite, need to be facilitated in order to relieve the enormous strain and stress that is placed on people caring for a loved one at home.

My part in Leigh's full-time care was, at times, exhausting. However, through his care I developed an inner strength and self-confidence while gaining invaluable knowledge and insight into his overall health and wellbeing. Throughout, I never lost sight of my most important role – being his mother.

★   ★   ★

The raw emotions that come from the death of a child, spouse or family member are ineffable.

Over time we somehow learn to live with these wretched feelings and to conceal the pain from those around us. We slowly come to terms with the fact that our lives are now changed forever, and struggle to find a new 'normal'. We carry on and keep the memories of our loved ones alive.

Through Leigh's immense courage, strength and determination, we now have a greater understanding of the meaning of love, joy and acceptance. We were always proud of Leigh's accomplishments through every milestone of his difficult life, and we will carry those treasured memories in our hearts and minds always.

"Life should not have been so difficult for such a precious soul."

Eulogy, Poems and Tributes

Eulogy

L eigh was a beautiful baby born on the twentieth day of November 1982, two years after his brother Jason. With big beautiful hazel eyes, long eyelashes and curls, he was often mistaken for a little girl as a baby. His eyes said it all and he used them to his full advantage, especially with me, his mother. A quiet-natured, thoughtful, loving child any mother would be proud of.

A day after his birth and the diagnosis of spina bifida, we began our long journey through the hospital system. A continual stream of hospital appointments, surgeries and therapy sessions became a way of life for our small family.

He was a 'hospital baby' now and I had to share him with strangers. For a long time I was envious of the hospital staff and the precious time they spent with Leigh: experiencing his first tooth appearing; his first taste of solid foods; and his reactions and facial expressions, first words and gestures. I missed everything during his early years! But I knew, deep down, the treatments and long stays away from home would give him a better chance at life and keep him well.

The precious time we had with him at home was a joy. He would make us laugh with his silly faces and we would be amazed at the advanced language skills he would pick up from medical staff during long stays in hospital. He would come out with some funny phrases that would stop us in our tracks. Later on he would shock us with his maths skills and mental calculations – he was a little whiz with numbers.

With the assistance of teacher aides and a modified school curriculum, he completed all levels of schooling and then continued on to Swinburne TAFE, where he obtained a Certificate I in Work Education.

In 2006, he started work at Nadrasca, where he quickly made close friends and acquaintances and was fully accepted into the supportive community. There he developed new skills and became more independent and confident in himself.

Nadrasca generously supplied an electric wheelchair for his work and this was a huge, exciting upgrade for Leigh because he could now go fast! I would often see him speeding along the corridors when I came to collect him. Occasionally, he would come home with a bruised arm from cutting the hallway corners at work! This was an exciting stage in his life and he loved belonging to a community.

He also enjoyed the social side of work – inviting colleagues over to play computer or Xbox games, and going to Nadrasca's Christmas parties and other social events. He was part of a supportive network.

Sport for Leigh was a challenge, but in his younger days, Leigh attended wheelchair basketball on Saturday mornings at Glen Waverley. Although he struggled to keep up with the pace, he would never complain and always persevered to help his team-mates win the game. He also loved his sports wheelchair and was disappointed when he was no longer able to use it.

Phillip, his father, would take him go-kart riding. Leigh also rode on a horse, sailed in a boat, and flew in a helicopter and on a plane. He also rode on some of the rides at Dream World and Luna Park that were wheelchair-friendly. Leigh was never excluded from family activities, as we wanted him to experience as much in life as he could in a safe and loving environment.

Leigh also used callipers during his younger years, but standing for long periods was daunting to him due to a fear of falling. He also had a swivel walker, whereby he could stand upright and twist his body to move forward, but this was a huge challenge for Leigh and, despite continued encouragement from everyone, he could not get over the fear of falling.

During later years, Leigh became very depressed and with-drawn after the sudden death of his father, Phillip. This event took a huge toll on the whole family, and he found strength and support from myself – his mother, Jason, Shanta and close work friends. Our family was small but we battled on alone. In time, with help and support, Leigh became more interested in the wrestling scene and attended a couple of WWE live events with his friend Simon. Leigh loved playing any wrestling Xbox or computer games and we would spend hours combing through computer stores looking for just the right game.

Leigh and Simon met when they attended Swinburne TAFE and worked together at Nadrasca. They continued to remain close friends, having similar interests and personalities. Simon was a huge support for Leigh in many ways.

As Leigh's health began to suffer, he unfortunately had to spend more time away from home and work. He would talk about how he missed his friends, home-life and his pets.

Leigh was in the process of receiving a new electric and manual wheelchair for home and work, and we would often talk about what colour to choose and how fast he could go ...

Leigh had a dedicated team of people eagerly waiting to start work on his new wheelchairs to give [him] a more comfortable and supportive seating system to make his life a little easier. But sadly, this never came to fruition.

I would like to thank all those people involved for their time, support and assistance over many years. Special thanks to Ms Christine Blackburn, Leigh's physiotherapist, for her long involvement with Leigh. And with much appreciation to Miss Elizabeth Lewis, Leigh's neurosurgeon, for her continued support and care during the many shunt revisions in the early days. To all the doctors, therapists, support care workers, work colleagues and friends – too many to name here in this short period – thank you from the bottom of my heart!

My darling son was taken too soon, too young; he struggled every day to be in this world and will now be reunited with his father and, one day, with me again.

Until we meet again, my sweetheart. I will always be

your loving mum.

My beautiful son, Leigh

Taken so quickly when I was not there
No time to say 'I love you', render aid or care.
You struggled every day and never thought to complain
Our shining light has left us
Our lives forever changed.
The disability you carried was so unfair and cruel
For one so kind and caring.
It left its mark on your body, but not on your beautiful heart
or soul.

Your daily struggle to keep up with life
Was vast and relentless
However, you carried on, surprising everyone you touched.

You showed me how to forgive myself
With your smile, your love and kisses
Dissolving the pain and anguish, I carried from my guilt.

Now free from pain and suffering
You are able to walk, fly and run
Whenever you wish to, my darling, loving son.
No barriers, no aides to use now
Any place, any time is yours to choose.

Till we meet again, my sweetheart
I will always be your caring, loving mum.

— *Charlene McIver*
21 October 2016

The first day after I said goodbye

My darling son, it's the first day after I said goodbye
My chest is heavy and my heart aches
Our routine is no more
No shopping trips to pass the time
No ham and cheese sandwiches to make
No more cups of cordial or tablets to take
How do I change our routine
when taking care of my beautiful son was my joy in life.
The rain and hail came today
And I worried about you lying there, scared and confused
in the cold and wet
Not understanding what had happened to you and why
you are there.
You remember lying in a hospital bed with your mask on,
maybe sleeping
Now, you are alone and confused in a perpetual state
of despair.
Maybe the TV was on and you were watching a movie
Maybe you could not sit up to get your drink
Maybe you could not reach the call button
for a nurse to attend
Maybe you did press the call button, but no one was there.
I struggle to comprehend and understand
what happened to you.
Oh my sweet boy
If only I knew
If only I knew you needed my help and I would have
been there.

I would tell you often how I would donate any part of my body
if it could help you, I would.
And that my love for you was forever.
I now live with the guilt of not being there to help you
on that night.

Your bedroom door is closed tonight and maybe I will go in
one day when I am stronger, to kiss you good night
and check on you.
But, for now the sounds of your voice remain embedded
in my heart forever and a day.

— *Charlene McIver*
22 October 2016

Tribute from Jason

(Leigh's brother)

Leigh was never given an equal opportunity, but he tried to maximise the ones he had. It was disappointing for him when things didn't work out as expected, but he never complained.

Leigh took on engineering traits from our dad and often had ideas of inventions to improve his own life. Some of his sketches included:

- 'A forklift for wheelchairs' – this would enable him to wheel himself into a forklift and lift large pallets to assist with his work at Nadrasca.

- 'A walking spider platform' – which resembled the Exoskeleton from the movie *Aliens*.

Due to his reduced mobility, video games were an escape for Leigh. He collected many games and his favourites were wrestling and car racing. When he was in the zone, you could hear from his bedroom the sounds of cars skidding, crowds cheering and the occasional cursing.

I sometimes joined him for a game or two, only to receive a couple of harsh lessons about wrestling I would not forget. A swift chair thrown in the back and the 'five knuckle shuffle' from his favourite character, John Cena. Before I could ask if that was an illegal move, he took a ladder to my face and clotheslined me over the ropes and onto the floor!

It was clear there was no way I could beat him at this game. Like his wheelchair and inventions, his player avatar was another extension of his body. We were not just playing video games; we were together in a world on the same playing field and it made me so happy, regardless of who won.

I miss you, Leigh, and our times we escaped together.

Love from your brother, Jason.

In memory of Leigh Thomas McIver

To hear your voice, to see your smile,
To sit and talk with you awhile
To be together in the same old way
Would be our wish today,
We laugh, we cry, we play our part
But behind it all lies broken hearts
We hide our tears when we speak your name,
Without you, life's not the same.
Our lives have only been enriched by knowing you, Leigh,
Our special nephew and cousin
Your infectious laugh – giggle – and that cheeky look
of simple pleasures,
Such memories are now our only treasures,
The few happy times we shared together,
Will be remembered with love forever.

— *the O'Brien family and Trevor*

My story about my nephew, Leigh Thomas McIver

It was a Sunday. I am talking about when my younger sister Charlene, with her husband Phillip and sons Jason and Leigh, came over to visit me. I was happy to see them. It was when Leigh was younger.

We had a nice lunch and I gave Leigh a lemonade drink with ice cream – a spider. I thought he would enjoy it, but a problem struck. It upset Leigh, who was then off to hospital. I felt like the silly Auntie Sylvia – 'What have I done?'

We loved you dear with good memories. Our special boy grew to be a young man with the love and care of his mother.

— Aunt Sylvia
(my eldest sister)

In honour of Leigh McIver

I cried the day I heard the news

My very special aunt gave birth to Leigh

Spina bifida, complications, the verdict was dim

His first day was the beginning of many days, weeks, months

in and out of hospital

Leigh quickly learned that many people would become a

vital role in his life

Doctors, nurses, family and friends

his most cherished love and support came from

his mother Charlene, father Phillip and brother Jason

Leigh's father passed away sadly from heart disease

Leigh remained a caring and compassionate soul for

his mother and brother

His struggle for survival became harder

His final month here was spent in hospital where it all began

He stayed until just after his mother's birthday

I cried the day I heard the news

Dearest Leigh

May you fly high and free

With love always,

your cousin Karen

(my eldest sister's daughter)

Tribute from Leigh's cousins

This book has been made with heartfelt love and compassion for a son from his mother. Any mother would understand the overwhelming love that you have for your child. The love stays with you forever. This book is about Leigh McIver, but I would like to specially mention Leigh's parents – Charlene and Phillip – and brother Jason. A passionate and devoted family that raised a wonderful gentle, lovable young man.

Leigh was the cutest baby, with such a beautiful smile and gorgeous curls. Growing up, I am sure Leigh faced many challenges as a teenager. But we never saw them. He only showed a positive and happy nature.

We are all very proud of what Leigh had achieved in his life and miss him dearly. I hope he is happy and watching over us with his dad by his side. We love you dearly and miss your beautiful smile.

Love from cousin Melinda, husband Gavin and family.

— *Melinda (my eldest sister's younger daughter)*

Tribute from Shanta
(a good friend)

Leigh was the kind of person who taught us all to be better human beings. He taught us courage, bravery and humility. He was a shining testament of how we all need to make time to be grateful for the simplest things in life.

It was such a delight when you saw Leigh smile, and that smile reached his beautiful eyes. There was nothing like it; that smile of his had the power to touch your heart with warmth, inspiration and, above all, love. He had such insurmountable obstacles to constantly overcome, but regardless, he always appreciated the smaller things in life, whether it be extra cheese on his favourite dish of spaghetti Bolognese, going on outings to Eastland for window shopping, playing video games with his friends, feeling the sun's warmth on his face and, most of all, being in the presence of loved ones. These moments he relished as a person and these moments he treasured immensely.

In the short time of his thirty-three years, he tried to live as best he could. There were many challenging times in his life, but he found a way to soldier on.

Leigh looked up to his older brother Jason, his number one fan. They had an unspeakable bond that nobody could ever break. Jason was Leigh's idol, his protector, his emotional strength. But even though Leigh admired Jason so much, it was Jason who looked up to his younger brother.

It was a great honour and a privilege to have known Leigh.

Love Shanta

Tribute from Simon

(Leigh's friend and work colleague)

I cannot believe you are gone. It seems like just yesterday that you and I were at TAFE and became best mates.

I will always remember your great personality and the many laughs we shared during our weekend hangouts.

You will always be my best friend and I will treasure what we had.

I love you, my brother, and goodbye.

Love Simon

Tribute from the Moyle family

(extended family on Phillip's side)

Thank you, Charlene, for the opportunity to share the Moyle family memories of Leigh. Fond memories, particularly from the early years when we saw Leigh and the family often. We all remember a warm, gorgeous, fun-loving boy who always had a smile – and a laugh – for everyone and who obviously enjoyed the company and interaction with those around him.

When we were all much younger, Mum and Dad loved spending time with the McIver family, always taking great interest in how everyone was going, playing games with Leigh and Jason, and catching up with Charlene and Phillip.

We remember Leigh playing with toys on the lounge room floor, having conversations with us, and very often surprising us with his understanding and depth of opinion, a demonstration of his strongly developing character.

In later years we know that Mum kept in contact with, and had a lot of time for, Charlene because Mum would always speak so highly of her respect for Charlene, doing so much for the entire family. She certainly knew that Charlene was a key part of who both Leigh and Jason had become because of Charlene's dedication and love – a love which certainly showed through from Leigh.

We have very fond memories of Leigh, happy and cheery, and always with a cheeky sparkle in his eyes to accompany that beautiful smile.

Tribute from Ms Christine Blackburn

(Consultant Physiotherapist)

I feel very privileged to speak with personal insight in regard to the medical issues that confronted both Leigh and his family. He attended the outpatient clinic for children with spina bifida. The clinic was different to anything we see today. It ran on a Saturday morning so that all the family could come: mums, dads, siblings and grandparents were welcome. The children and their families would occupy one of the clinical rooms in Outpatients, turning up whenever it suited them. The staff would rotate through the rooms. There was always a cup of coffee or tea outside in the corridor, so the families often joined together to talk around the shared issues of having a child with a disability. So many families gave the staff insight into management strategies for their children, and we in turn shared these ideas with other families as the years rolled on. So the clinic realised many things: educating the staff around how families coped with a child with a disability, as well as creating 'shared experiences' for the families.

The highlight of the clinic mornings were the children – all with varying levels of disability, but all with bright smiles and the cheekiest dispositions. Many children mobilised in a variant of a wheelchair, called the chariot, from the young age of ten months or so. We were surrounded by the oddest pieces of equipment, aids to helping them sit, stand or move. Many built by the dads, some designed by mums, made out of wood, steel and often things such as golf buggy wheels.

All of these children had amazingly bright personalities. Often, because of their physical disability, their language developed early and, like Leigh, the outstanding thing about all of them was that they ignored the physical limitations of their disability and got on with being a child. We recognised, as the families did, that the great thing about being an innocent child with a disability is that you never picture yourself as an adult with a disability. You just believe you will grow up and be like everyone else. Hence your childhood can still be fun, for most of the time, except when you're in hospital!

The kids in the clinic would visit each other's rooms, often going missing when the 'orthopod' or neurosurgeon came visiting. The challenge for the older kids was to raid the back area where the coffee and snacks were (for the staff) and to sneak off with a bit of cake. The trail of crumbs and the bright eyed 'mucky hands and faces' often gave the culprits away.

Leigh came into the clinic at around eight years of age after being managed at Queen Vic by Miss Lewis and having experienced surgery to close his spine as an infant. He had many shunt revisions during his childhood, but soon had to endure the world of spinal surgery.

His visits to the clinic explored the tough times he was having with his spine. He had a very complicated hip, pelvic and spinal alignment and I think we all empathised with the frustration that Charlene and Phillip felt when sometimes nothing seemed to go well. I remember Phillip standing in the clinic and just about exploding as he recounted an episode at the hospital. Leigh had been prepped for surgery, but was then given breakfast by a nurse. The episode ended with Leigh in ICU.

Phillip stood in the clinic, exploding with disbelief that it could have happened, recounting the episode to staff while we all stood there thinking, 'Maybe it could have happened here?'

The outcomes of his surgery always seemed to be unpredictable. A spinal rod was inserted with fixation across the pelvis, but his pelvic bones 'melted' around the fixing rod so it had to be removed. A spinal fusion followed but that only worked for a limited section of his spine.

Miss Lewis remarked, 'Leigh was one of the toughest cases to manage and with all the best techniques in the world; the spine is still the most problematic surgery to get a positive outcome. This is especially true for those children and adults with SB, where the underlying deformity is so complex.'

I think the outstanding thing that we all remember was Leigh's quiet sense of self. He seemed to travel through these dilemmas with a calmness that probably belied his anxiety and that of his parents.

He had a grin that would peep through when you asked, 'How are you going?'

'Alright,' he'd say. A man of not many words.

Anyone who knows me well knows that I have a problem tolerating a health system that fails large numbers of our community, especially those who have a disability. As with all children with a disability, the time comes when they have to transition into adult services. It is with complete frustration that, despite initial optimism, transition services have proven that they are not purpose-built to manage those with a disability. Leigh missed out on the transition services by being too old when they came into being. Today, transition clinics provide a limited service for only two to three years for each patient, so those young adults with complex disabilities end up transitioned into mainstream health services that fail to cope with their emerging needs as adults. Very few of our health services have the experience in their staff to cope with the specific needs of a patient like Leigh. This has been a total frustration for Charlene.

Over the last few months I became engaged again with Leigh around obtaining an electric wheelchair that would manage his needs and give him some independence. I visited him at Nadrasca, his workplace, and it struck me on that day that he had not changed through the years. He was still that quiet young man with a self-contained dignity about him. He did not want to 'rock any boats', despite the fact that he had so many issues that needed attention. It became obvious that day that it would take a very complex seating system to assist in keeping him comfortable.

The frustration is still there for me – that what should have been a simple process in a first-world country like Australia took so long. It was the team from the inner east that eventually managed his case, outside of their normal catchment area; they took up the challenge not only to assist with getting the right chair, but also all the funding needed. These wheelchairs cost around $25000, the cost of a new car for most people. It all came together ten weeks ago.

However, the events of the last few weeks and months have intervened, and so Leigh was not to get the chair that would give him the ability to move around with comfort and ease under his own control.

He was a young man with great humility who wore his disability with grace and dignity. So often we ask why this should happen to one individual. I don't think any of us can answer that question honestly.

To mourn too long for those we love is self-indulgent but to honour their memory with a promise to live life a little better for having known them, gives purpose to their life and some reason for their death.

— *The Thoughts of Nanushka*, Nan Whitcomb

I think that applies to all of us who knew Leigh. He made us all better human beings for having known him.

Thank you for the privilege to speak about Leigh.

Tribute from Nadrasca

Leigh worked on various packing and assembly tasks at Nadrasca.

He was always keen to be treated like everyone else and was prepared to give anything a go. Because of this he worked on a wide variety of tasks over the years.

At the end of the day, Leigh would grab a broom and help to clean up; he did not see there was any reason he could not help! And he did a good job, too.

He enjoyed the use of an electric wheelchair at work and was very adept at manoeuvring and adjusting the height and position to suit the tasks he worked on. Except when going through doorways – we were constantly reminding him to pull his elbow in!

We also needed to remind him to use his drink bottle, but he never appeared annoyed – he was very tolerant and patient with us and our nagging!

Leigh found using his electric wheelchair outdoors very challenging, however. We spent some time helping him to gain confidence, and on a few occasions he was able to collect mail from the post office and visit a local café. This was challenging for Leigh, as he found uneven surfaces quite scary. This proved to be a great achievement for him, overcoming his fear and being more independent.

Leigh was quietly spoken at work; he enjoyed a chat and a laugh with his friends here and he was well liked by all.

He will be missed.

Leigh started working at Nadrasca in October 2006. We would like to present him with his Ten Year Service Award Certificate for his work at Nadrasca.

— *Leigh's supervisor*

ABOUT THE AUTHOR

Charlene is a compassionate, pragmatic and determined individual who has coped with heartache many of us do not wish to imagine.

Her younger son, Leigh, was diagnosed with a disability soon after birth. Throughout his life, Charlene cared for Leigh and advocated for him in every aspect of his life, including his interactions with the hospital system. In 2008 she lost her loving husband of thirty-two years and, in 2016, she endured the loss of Leigh. She has found strength in writing this biography and hopes it will help others who are raising, or caring for, a child or adult with a disability.

When they found the time, Charlene and her late husband Phillip enjoyed frequenting antique shops and fairs. They were keen gardeners and designed their garden around a fountain and an antique iron gate, which they lovingly restored. She also established a widows' support group in her local community following the sudden passing of her husband, which still gathers.

Charlene has a background in accounting, but her real passion is in natural therapies: she has studied herbal medicine, remedial massage, aromatherapy, clinical hypnotherapy, and more. This was her way of coping with stress and it also brought other areas of interest into their family's life.

After the sudden loss of Leigh, she set about instigating changes to a Melbourne hospital's end-of-life policy and procedures. Although only small changes were initiated, she believes they will make a difference to anyone having to deal with the experience of losing a loved one.

CONTACTS

Access Health and Community
Phone: (03) 9810 3000
Website: accesshc.org.au

Australian Centre for Grief and Bereavement
Phone: (03) 9265 2100
Email: info@grief.org.au
Website: www.grief.org.au

Beyond Blue (Depression, Anxiety)
Phone: 1300 224 636
Website: www.beyondblue.org.au

Compassionate Friends Australia, The
Supporting grandparents, parents and siblings after a child dies
Phone: 1300 064 068
Website: www.tcfaustralia.org.au

Hydrofera Blue foam dressing
Hollister Wound Care
2000 Hollister Drive
Libertyville, IL 60048 USA
Website: www.hollisterwoundcare.com

Interchange Incorporated
Level 7, 225 Bourke Street
Melbourne Vic. 3000
Phone: (03) 9663 4886
      1300 300 436 (free call)
Email: enquiries@interchange.org.au

Lifeline Australia

Phone: 13 11 14 (24-hours)

Website: www.lifeline.org.au

Nadrasca

52–62 Rooks Road

Nunawading Vic. 3131

Phone: (03) 9873 1111

Email: nadrasca@nadrasca.com.au

RDNS

Phone: 1300 334 455

SCOPE

Level 2, 302 Burwood Road

Hawthorn Vic. 3122

Phone: 1300 472 673

Website: www.scopeaust.org.au

Spina Bifida Foundation Victoria

Level 4, Ross House

247 Flinders Lane

Melbourne Vic. 3000

Phone: (03) 9663 0075

Email: info@sbfv.org.au

Widows and Widowers Support Group (Croydon)

Glenn Frost Room, Croydon Library

Civic Square

Croydon Vic. 3136

(can be contacted only through the Australian Centre for
 Grief and Bereavement listed above)

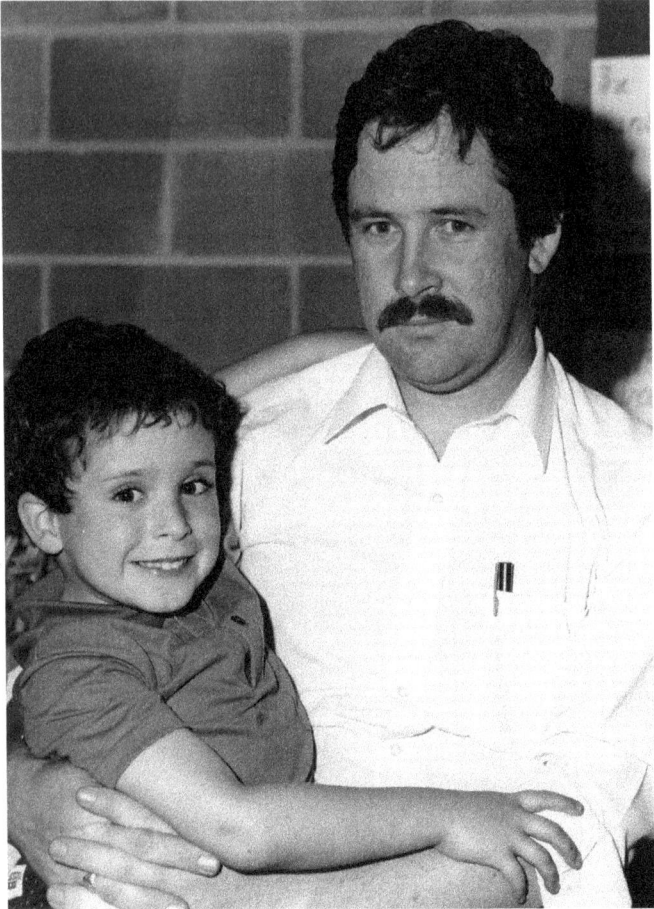

Leigh's drawing of two angels meeting at a golden gate (age unknown). It was discovered after his passing.

www.ingramcontent.com/pod-product-compliance
Lightning Source LLC
Chambersburg PA
CBHW041257040426
42334CB00028BA/3057